The proceeds from this publication are intended for the purposes of research and education of prison administration, the transplant community and the general public of the modern realities and benefits of prisoner organ donations. Neither the author nor any prisoner will benefit monetarily from this publication.

LETHAL REJECTION

THE FIGHT TO GIVE LIFE FROM PRISONS AND OTHER POINTLESSLY FORBIDDEN PLACES

BY CHRISTIAN M. LONGO

CONpendium Publishers - Copyright 2014

ISBN-13: 978-0692329269

LETHAL REJECTION

THE FIGHT TO GIVE LIFE FROM PRISONS AND OTHER POINTLESSLY FORBIDDEN PLACES

Christian M. Longo

THIS BOOK IS DEDICATED TO THE ONE WHO MOTIVATED A WISH TO MAKE A MIGHTY OAK RISE FROM A CRUSHED ACORN. WITHOUT YOU, THIS JOURNEY WOULD NEVER HAVE BEEN MADE.

<}

CONTENTS

Prologue

Salem, Oregon. November 29

Shari's heart was failing fast.

She stares in annoyance at another old episode of something she never would have watched in the first place if it weren't for being trapped in this hospital room... again. It wasn't the exact same room, but it might as well have been. They all started to look the same after so many stays. It was fitting enough for a home away from home, she supposed. Although, it could come with a better view than the giant Douglas fir tree standing 10 feet from her window, completely obstructing the sight of everything but branches. The sun couldn't break through. It always seemed dark. There was the relentless slow Oregon rain. There weren't even any birds chirping. Was it possible that it could be drearier outside than it was inside a hospital room?

"Probably not," Shari whispered, in between the short, quick gasps of her labored breathing. The worrisome, forceful, irregular thumping of her straining heart against her chest wall didn't help her depressed view. Her body felt like it was always trying to decide if it wanted to be excited. At least the thumping distracted her from her earlier thoughts of looking at the IV's tethering her arms to the pole that was anchored to her bed, which was permanently mounted to the hospital floor. It was as if she were now at the end of a vine in a big garden that grew nothing but sickness and death.

She wasn't normally quite this half-empty-glass of a woman. She wasn't exactly a hyper-optimistic sort either. She was more the one who would encounter life's sinkholes and step on the gas to power through them before they could swallow her whole. It wasn't positivity or negativity. It was simply necessity. As a single mom of a two teenagers - one of each variety - her world was too hectic to let anything get in her way. Life was literally too short. But she wasn't unreasonable. She didn't need fifty more years, or even another thirty-eight. So long as she made it to both of her babies-grown-up graduations and got to kiss them on their way into college, she reasoned that her life would be complete. Well, maybe that and the opportunity to cuddle with a grandchild or two. But she was usually kind of torn on that one.

Today, she was frustrated at having to spend another uncertain week in the hospital, right before a holiday again, three days in and at least three days more than she felt she needed. If left to her own will, she would put the pedal to the floor and speed out of this hole. She had work to get to, funds to earn to spend on the Christmas presents -- not to mention to pay the bills that refused to have the courtesy to stop when she had to. But the doctors had told her that this was one hole that would consume her if she didn't apply the brakes immediately. Of course, "immediately" was months ago. She stopped when the wheels almost fell off, as was her way. This time, though, it may have been too late.

It came with the territory. She was used to it. The times in between her hospital stays were dotted with the usual life pleasures and pains. The pleasures, every moment she got with her young woman of a daughter and her baby boy of 15 years. The pains: work, car troubles, unexpected hassles - anything that threatened the potential for mom moments, which seemed far too frequent these days. Unfortunately, her "usual" also included pharmaceutical refills, daily injections, every other day trips and stays at her real home-away-from-home, the dialysis clinic. Three days a week, life was forced to pause so that another vine growing from that garden of illness could suck out the toxins that built up in her blood the day before. She had a love/hate relationship with the dialysis machine she called Norton. Norton extended her life, but it also made her sick. Every other day she was more ill than usual -- a cruel teeter-totter of anguish.

Ten years ago, doctors gave her seven to nine years to live with a condition that would literally harden her organs to a point of uselessness. Some called it the Medusa disease. The disorder came with a grab bag of hassles that would manifest themselves in all sorts of obnoxious ways. From fingertips that felt frostbitten and constant fatigue, to migraines that shots could barely soften anymore, and a steady stream of organ malfunctions. Anything in between was merciful. But it was the autoimmune nature of the condition that made life most difficult. Most hospital stays were for pneumonia, or for some other ailment she just couldn't heal from without stopping for a professional healer's expertise. It was a usual criticism from the doctor that Shari was hurting more today because she played chicken with the sinkhole a bit too long. But to her, she didn't squeeze enough seconds out to do what she felt was more important.

For the last couple of years, it was her kidneys that threatened to stop her permanently. They had nearly zero functionality. The doctors had said something like 7%. Dialysis was her compromise. Those hours trapped with Norton added days that she could spend with her two prizes. But that compromise was quickly becoming an option she could no longer count on either. Where most on dialysis can stay on it forever, or until a better kidney becomes available from a matching donor, this machine was simultaneously helping her survive and killing her. Each session was taking more out of her than her slow-to-heal body could recover from. Now her kidneys were no longer her greatest problem. Three days ago, 45 minutes after her time with Norton, she collapsed from a heart attack.

She needed a kidney and now possibly a heart. But a kidney was the priority. One that wasn't made of stone would alleviate the stresses on her body caused by dialysis... at least long enough to see her babies graduate. It wasn't as simple as just finding a matching donor to give her the part she needed, though - which was a formidable obstacle in itself. Because of her underlying disorder, with its inability to let her heal normally, and its unpredictable waves of other problems, she wasn't exactly a prime candidate for such a major surgery. She was certainly not well enough to be added to the national waiting list for kidneys, at least not for anything longer than temporary appearances. But even if she could stay on the list, the average wait is longer than 3 years. She wouldn't last that long. Without a new kidney, though, she might not last the rest of the year. The cruelest kind of catch-22.

There was a slim hope that if a willing donor appeared, who happened to be the same blood type and was a close enough match, and if she could stay healthy enough for long enough to get the okay from the transplant doctors to try the transplant, she might be able to get her reprieve. She'd had healthy enough bouts before. It could happen. She was a believer.

But for now, she had no choice but to stay on dialysis and weather whatever cropped up. It was dire, but not absolute. She could still make it, she hoped. Her oldest was a senior, with her youngest close behind. She just needed a couple more years to make it to both graduations. Then it could have her. She wouldn't actively seek a donor. As a believer, it would happen if it were meant to be. Besides, it seemed selfish to her, knowing that there was a waiting list a hundred miles long. She saw several of the line-waiters sitting next to her every other day. She'd be taking from them. No, she would just do the best she could with the hand dealt to her, and pray she'd make it to her hopeful finish line.

--

A quiet guilty pleasure of Shari's was to watch and read anything true-crime. Whether it was reading about a tragedy far worse than anything she would ever experience, making her woes somehow not seem quite so woeful, or if it was just entertaining to her on some morbid level, she didn't know. She just knew that it passed the far too many hours when she was trapped by her illness.

One extended weekend, shortly after the diagnosis of her condition, while laid up for another healing hospital session, she noticed the unavoidable front-page headline of the local paper, "DEATH: Guilty on All Seven Capital Murder Charges!" She already knew the story. She even figured that this would be the outcome. Her true-crime reading usually came in the form of novels, not the local papers. But this one happened only an hour away, near the exact locations in the same coastal town that she liked to take her kids to during healthy weekends getaways, and it was plastered all over the local and national news. She couldn't help but pay attention.

Something else drew her to the story too, though. Something less tangible than she could quite put her finger on. It might have been that the accused murderer seemed like the normal guy-next-door, completely unassuming and safe-looking enough. She might have gone out to dinner with him in another time, shared a dessert of baklava under different circumstances. Maybe it was simply that it was a local connection to somebody who would likely be the subject of one of her true-crime novels or even a movie someday. Whatever it was, she couldn't stop thinking about him, until one day she decided to do something she had never even considered doing before. She wrote him on death row.

There was no real motive behind her writing him. She wasn't really clear on her reasons herself. It certainly wasn't to talk about her health conditions, or to see if he happened to have a kidney he wouldn't mind parting with. Perhaps it was just to find a place to dump all of the anxieties and toxins of her week, kind of like a human dialysis machine. Her personal listening Norton. She could say whatever she needed to onto paper to be read by the eyes of somebody who was safely boxed away, who probably had nothing better to do than to read what others sent him. Maybe that was it, simply a release valve.

Whatever it was, she didn't have any real expectations. She certainly didn't expect to form any sort of bond with the guy, or a friendship that she would be comfortable enough in to share her deepest of life's pros and woes. But somehow the unexpected happened. They became friends, at times even voicing and believing that they were each other's best friends, the most trusted sort. Each other's confidants. It wasn't a romantic thing really, not like what you see on documentary exposés on 'love from behind bars'. But it was certainly some sort of a companionship -- an unusual one for sure.

No one would understand the relationship they had formed. Most would assume that he was manipulating her for his own needs, for a connection with the outside world that could send him money for prison canteen, or whatever else he needed for a better life in a concrete box. But she never gave him a dime, and he never asked. Others would assume that her fascination with a murderer was brought about by some mental disorder or perverse curiosity. But she quickly stopped thinking about his crime, and thought of him simply as a friend. Possibly her best friend. Whatever this unconventional thing was, it was one that worked for them.

He knew about her condition. He knew every time she got sick. She told him more than she'd meant to, more than she'd told most anyone else in her life. She knew that it was torturous for him to be helpless to do anything to fix it, to make her life easier, or the pains less. But even despite her thinking less about his crimes, she knew he deserved to be there for doing the terrible that he had done. It made her sad, but she tried to be lighthearted about it. It became sort of a running joke with them that he deserved whatever pains he suffered from his confines, like every time she told him she was eating something that he craved, or the latest movie that she just went to see without him. Not being able to help her was just something he had to deal with. It was ~~of~~ his punishment, she'd tell him. "And whose fault is that," she'd say. "You made your bed."

What she didn't know was that he was dealing with it in a different way than she expected. From the day she told him of her health condition, he began researching everything he could on it. He ordered books, subscribed to the foundation newsletters of the advocates working on cures for her particular malfunctions, unearthing any information he could gather on all things that adversely affected her. Every new up-cropping ailment would be quickly looked up and studied until he knew more about it than she did.

Soon he began requesting information from his prison system concerning the option of being tested for organ donation. He knew that she would need a transplant to make it much further on this earth, even though she often tried to keep the severity of things from him. He figured, without her ever considering raising the subject, that if it turned out that he was a match, he would easily gift her the kidney that his body didn't need. He was healthy, adamant about maintaining his health for that reason more than any other, especially once he knew that he might actually be able to help her. He was more than willing enough to gift her whatever part she may need. It would be his unquestionable pleasure. Whatever the hurdles, he was prepared to start making the arrangements as soon as the prison told him how to go about it.

Only, the prison turned out to be the most substantial roadblock of all – as if the walls were there for the purpose of ensuring that no part of him would make it beyond them. They would not allow him to donate to Shari, or anyone else for that matter. There was some potential to be able to donate to a blood relative, but as he would quickly learn, even that wasn't likely, under current prison and transplant community regulations.

Needless to say, he was crushed. If it would work to rip his kidney out and send it to her in a priority mailer, he would have. But it wasn't a viable option. It was absurd, he knew. But he had no power from a prison cell. He made his bed. He didn't even know whether he was a good match for her to receive his kidney in the first place. But the prison wouldn't allow him to even get the testing to find out. Even if he were, though, they wouldn't let him donate. He was discouraged, angry... infuriated. The walls had never seemed so high or so thick.

In his usual way, with nothing left to do, he began researching the issue. It was under his skin now. It bugged him. One positive, or negative, depending on your perspective, about being stuck in a tiny box for most of every day is that it hyper-focuses you, to a point of obsession if you let it. It's what reforms some, or makes others more proficient criminals. For him, he needed to know why organ donations from prisoners were not allowed. He wrote hundreds of letters, asking every related government agency and regulator, procurement center, transplant and health authority, prison group... anyone he could think of who would tell him why inmates could not give organs or tissue to help someone in need. He got plenty of crumbs that led to still more exploration and inquiry, which led to even more research. Before long, he had the 'reasons', which he quickly grew to thinking of as excuses. Before long, he began to realize just how outdated and life threatening their rationale for prohibiting prisoner organ and tissue donors really was. The transplant and prison policies against such donations were literally and needlessly costing lives... quite possibly the life of his best friend.

Obsession turned to passion. From that point on it became his mission to do everything in his shackled power to force the prison and transplant industry into taking a real look at this issue. It became his drive to find a way to change the rule so that Shari and the other Shari's of the world might have another option at life that they might not be able to find elsewhere.

Whether Shari will be able to fight long enough to survive the sinkhole that threatens to consume her, to be able to make it to her life goal of being at her children's graduation, remains to be seen. But if her imprisoned friend is successful, turning out to be the unexpected answer to her prayers, she may be able to not only reach her goal, but one day be able to meet her children's children, and to be the grandmother she wasn't so sure she wanted to be... which she'd savor every moment of.

Likewise, too, anyone else who needs an organ to survive may be able to gain life from this unlikely source – a surprisingly large number of willing inmate donors who have already stepped forward to offer organs and tissue to those who may die without them. Tens of thousands of prisoners would like nothing better than to be able to have the good fortune of doing something positive from their otherwise unfortunate circumstances. There is no greater opportunity for any human – caged or not –– nor any greater gift or satisfaction than to be able to save a life. To prevent this because the donor happens to live behind bars is a pointless and tragic waste of life.

WHAT'S THE BIG DEAL?

FACTS:
24
THE TOTAL OF AMERICANS, ON AVERAGE, WHO WILL DIE TODAY AND EVERY DAY WAITING FOR AN ORGAN OR TISSUE TRANSPLANT.
121,000

THE NUMBER OF AMERICANS CURRENTLY ON ORGAN TRANSPLANT WAITING LISTS.

(AS OF JANUARY 2014)

13,900

THE NUMBER OF AMERICANS CURRENTLY ON BONE MARROW WAITING LISTS

(AS OF JANUARY 2014)

60

THE MINUTES FROM NOW THAT SOMEBODY ELSE WILL DIE UNNECESSARILY FOR LACK OF A NEEDED ORGAN, BONE MARROW OR OTHER TISSUE IN THE U.S.

INTRODUCTION

Eight years ago, I was sentenced to death for the murders of my wife and three children. I am guilty. I cannot take that back. I will die for what I did.

When I die, my organs will go to waste because the prison and the transplant community will not allow me to donate them. My organs are healthy. My body alone can save eight lives or many more, and mine isn't the only one.

There are over 2 million prisoners in the U.S. Many of those try to find positive ways to improve their lives. Some seek to do so through organ or tissue donation. However, as I've learned while trying to donate my own organs, almost all prisoners are effectively banned from such donations, either while alive or after death. That's especially so for the dozens who are forced to die every year, death row prisoners who, like myself, are stuck with a fate of death by lethal injection. Many of us, more than half as recent surveys show, likewise wish to be able to do something positive from our circumstances with what we have left. If that can only come at the absolute end, while facing our sentence, so be it. Let us donate.

There are over 135,000 people currently dying on organ and bone marrow waiting lists in the U.S. The transplant community cannot supply enough organs to keep up with the need. We can help. If a healthy prisoner wants to part with a kidney or donate bone marrow by his own request while he is alive, without any incentives to do so, he should be able to. Furthermore, there should certainly be no excuses for preventing a healthy prisoner from donating life after he dies. Let us be organ donors and save lives. If allowed, we would drastically reduce the organ shortage crisis in this country.

It is as simple as that, but as you will see, many would have you think otherwise.

The first hurdle for organ donation from prisoners rests on prison directors, the governor appointed gatekeepers who determine prison policies. However, due to the prison systems reluctance to stray from the status quo, regardless of its potential impact for the community, getting prison authorities to permit such donations is a challenge. One prison Director summed up the disconnect between apprehension to change and the needs of the community in response to my petitions to donate when he said, "Upon consideration of the legal, operational, social and policy implications...the interest of the public and condemned inmates are best served by denying the petition." The public, inmates, and especially those dying for lack of a healthy organ or tissue would disagree, and I can prove it.

In response to the denials of my wishes to donate after execution I wrote an op-ed piece that was chosen by the New York Times for publishing in their March 6th, 2011 Sunday edition. It elicited a tremendous amount of response from the public and professionals on all sides of this issue. Many reacted emotionally to 'the likes of me' offering such a thing or for getting such valuable print space to air my complaint. Some impulsively stated what they felt were obvious roadblocks to prisoner organ donations, challenges the average person might assume. Others gave impassioned responses that, without knowing it, provided logic that was provable through sufficient research. Still others felt that it just made sense and were surprised to learn that such donations were not already happening.

Even if we could get past the prison administrators on the road to donation, the transplant community presents an even bigger hurdle. It quickly became clear in the responses to my article that transplant policy-makers are strictly opposed to prisoner organ donations – especially those that come from a death row inmate. A surprising revelation, however, was that the rest of those in the transplant profession – the non-policy-makers – are completely divided on this issue. There were even fervent opinions from transplant colleagues in identical positions at the same hospital who held polarized opinions as to whether such donations are right or wrong. If they cannot agree with each other, how likely is it that a man on death row will be successful in single-handedly influencing the decision-makers that he should be able to donate? The answer is that I can't. That is why I've written this. This is my attempt to put the issue out there as thoroughly as possible to generate enough support to change the prison and transplant communities' stance, as well as to further bolster the already positive public view of the potential for prisoner organ and tissue donation.

This book is written for those who want to know more about why prisoner organ donation is not already occurring, or who think they do. Whether, you need an organ or want to give one, whether you work in the transplant community or criminal justice system, or if you simply find this topic worth considering, this is a vital read.

With such a rift in opinions, the only way to potentially build a bridge between prisoners and those who could benefit from their freely offered parts is with a complete and detailed picture and reason. I don't presume to be able to tell the transplant community or the prisons anything that they do not know or have access to. I only hope to bring attention to the information at their disposal, as well as to the issues and concerns in a light that they may not have honestly considered - from the vantage point of those who need an organ to survive, and a death row inmate who has admitted his guilt and wishes to donate his healthy organs and tissue.

The chapters that follow each raise and debate a popular stated concern as to why such organ donations should not occur. The scientific data has been verified independently and is completely referenced for transparency. However, I am completely biased in my belief that organ donation from prisoners should be allowed so long as the prisoner is absolutely willing, healthy and capable. To disallow this, especially in light of the research and those dying is, to me, absurd.

Thank you for your consideration of this life-saving concern.

Christian M. Longo

christianlongo@gavelife.org

WHAT DO PRISONS CURRENTLY ALLOW?

_____

_____

_____

FACTS:

1

TOTAL NUMBER OF STATES THAT LEGISLATIVELY ALLOWS PRISONERS TO
SIGN UP AS ORGAN DONORS.

(UTAH – NEW LAW INSTATED MARCH 2013)

5

THE NUMBER OF STATE PRISON SYSTEMS THAT CURRENTLY HAVE
WRITTEN POLICIES ALLOWING INMATES TO DONATE ORGANS OR TISSUE...
BUT ONLY TO FAMILY MEMBERS.

(TEXAS, OHIO, WISCONSIN, ARIZONA, CALIFORNIA)

0

THE TOTAL OF STATE PRISONS THAT EXPLICITLY ALLOW PRISONERS TO
DONATE TO STRANGERS OR NON–FAMILY MEMBERS.

(OUT OF 51 PRISON SYSTEMS)

CHAPTER 1

The History of Organ Transplantation & the Donor Shortage

Would you be surprised to learn that successful human transplants have been happening since about the time that Abraham Lincoln was the U.S. President? It's true. Transplantation has had a relatively long history. Perhaps not so surprisingly, however, were the substantial roadblocks that had to be navigated to even get to the point of the first successful transplant, some of which continue to present challenges today.

There are actually several accounts of transplantation from centuries before Honest Abe's time, although most are more of a mythical nature, coming from times before the possibility of scientific understanding and advancements that would have been necessary for them to have realistically occurred. In one of the earliest examples, a Chinese physician by the name of Pien Chi'ao reportedly performed the first heart transplant. The legend goes that he took the heart of a man of strong spirit but weak will and exchanged it with one of a man of weak spirit but strong will in an attempt to achieve a proper balance in each man. Unsurprisingly, there are no reports of whether either recipient survived.

Okay, so perhaps we can't add that to the actual history of transplantation. Let's try this one. Roman Catholic accounts report the first leg transplant as happening around the 300 A.D, a good sixteen centuries before modern medicine figured it out. Performed by two third-century saints, Damian and Cosmas, testimonials claim that they replaced the gangrenous leg of a Roman deacon Justinian with the leg of a recently deceased Ethiopian. In case you might be prone to give some credence to the possibility that this actually may have happened, you should know that most accounts have the saints performing the transplant closer to 400 A.D., decades after their deaths. However, some accounts do have them merely teaching the living surgeons who actually performed the procedure, which they of course had to do the instructing from a spiritual plane of existence.

Getting to more likely accounts of early transplants, the more realistic possibilities of early transplantation deal with a much bigger, but less fragile organ – the skin. The first reasonable account is of the Indian surgeon Suthruta who, in the second century B.C., reportedly used skin transplantation in a nose reconstruction. Success or failure of the procedure is not well documented, which might mean that it didn't go so well. However, centuries later, the Italian surgeon Gasparo Tagliacozzi did perform the first documented successful skin transplant from one part of his patient's body to another – the first known, successful skin autograft. Although, it is also well documented that he consistently failed when trying to transplant skin from donors onto his patients, but these failures offered the first suggestion of rejection from non–matching donors centuries before the mechanism could possibly be understood. Incidentally, he attributed the failures to the "force and power of individuality" in his 1596 work De Cortorum Chirurgia per Institionem.

It wasn't until 1869 that the first successful allograft skin transplant from a donor was documented, just four years after President Lincoln abruptly left office. However, major leaps in skin transplantation did not really occur until the First World War, notably in the work of Harold Gillies at Aldershot. Among his advances was the tubed pedicle graft. He figured out a way of maintaining a flesh connection from the donor site until the graft could establish its own blood flow, thus making it more likely that the transplant would be successful. Gillies' assistant, Archibald Melndoe, carried on the work into the Second World War as a notable reconstructive surgery.

If skin transplantation is not exciting enough, the first successful eye-related transplant, a corneal allograft, was performed in 1837; but it was in a gazelle. The first successful human corneal transplant wasn't performed until much later, in 1905, by Eduard Zirm of the Czech Republic.

One of the major hurdles preventing successful transplantation had to do with the connecting of the donor organs in a way that the body could accept them as their own. Pioneering work in this area was finally made in the early 1900's, by the French surgeon Alexis Carrel and Charles Guthrie. Their work concerned the transplantation of arteries and veins, through the development of new suturing techniques. Their skillful operations laid the groundwork for all later successful transplant surgery, even winning Carrel the 1912 Nobel Prize in Physiology of Medicine. He would later prove to have additional accomplishments through transplant experimentation on dogs. Surgically successful in moving kidneys, hearts and spleens, he was one of the first to identify the problem of organ and tissue rejection.

The rejection issue remained insurmountable for decades. The first attempted human deceased-donor transplant was performed by the Ukrainian surgeon Yu Yu Vorono in the 1930's; however, rejection quickly resulted in failure. In the late 1940's, Peter Medawar, working for the National Institute of Medical Research, improved the understanding of rejection, suggesting that immunosuppressive drugs might be the answer. Cortisone had been recently discovered and it was hoped that this could open the field of successful transplantation dramatically. The more effective azathioprine was identified in 1959, however, there continued to be problems with rejection through the 1950s and 60s.

Joseph Murray, as lead surgeon, and J. Hartwell Harrison, M.D. performed the first successful kidney transplant, a transplant between identical twin brothers Ronald and Richard Herrick, in 1954. Ronald's kidney donation extended his brothers life by another eight years, in which time Richard was able to enjoy life with his new bride – whom he'd met, incidentally, as a nurse stationed in his transplant recovery room. Ronald himself just recently passed at the age of 79, surviving 56 years after the surgery.

Even though it was before the advent of the necessary immunosuppressive drugs, their transplant was so successful because of the identical genetic makeup as twins; rejection was not an issue. At the age of 91, Dr. Murray, reflecting back on the surgery, stated in a recent interview, "This operation rejuvenated the whole field of transplantation." It did indeed, encouraging a mass of attempts with every other major organ. It also happened to win Dr. Murray a Nobel Prize.

Success was not immediately achieved, however. There was limited success with a deceased-donor lung transplant into a lung cancer sufferer in June 1963 by James Hardy in Jackson, Mississippi. However, the patient only survived for eighteen days before finally succumbing to kidney failure. Thomas Starzl of Denver attempted a liver transplant in the same year, but did not prove to be successful until 1967.

The heart was the Holy Grail for transplant surgeons, though. But, in addition to the still-challenging rejection issues, the heart didn't last long once it was removed from the donor. It deteriorated within minutes of death, so any operation had to be performed very quickly. Lung pioneer James Hardy attempted a human heart transplant in 1964, but a premature failure of the recipient's heart caught Hardy with no human donor. Instead, he tried transplanting a heart from an unsuspecting chimpanzee, which failed very quickly.

Christiaan Barnard in Cape Town, South Africa finally achieved the first success December 3, 1967. Louis Washkansky, the recipient, survived for eighteen days amid what many saw as a distasteful publicity circus. However, the media interest prompted a spate of heart transplants. Over a hundred were performed in 1968-69, but most all patients died within sixty days. Barnard's second patient, Philip Blaiberg, managed to live for nineteen months.

It wasn't until the discovery of cyclosporine in 1970 that transplant surgery truly found a sufficiently powerful immunosuppressive that could take transplants from research surgery to life-saving treatment, as we know it today. In 1968, surgical pioneer Denton Cooley performed seventeen transplants including the first heart-lung transplant. Fourteen of those patients were dead within six months. But by 1984, two-thirds of all heart transplant patients survived for five years or more.

From then on, organ transplants started to become commonplace. Limited only by donors, surgeons moved onto more risky fields, like multiple organ transplants on humans and whole-body transplant research on animals. On March 9, 1981, the first successful combined heart and lung transplant took place at Stanford University Hospital.

As the rising success rate of transplants and modern immunosuppression made transplants more common, the need for more organs became critical. Today, organ transplantation has become a common fix for many chronic disorders, making the shortage of available organs the biggest issue for the transplant professionals to overcome. Every year thousands die whom a now common organ or tissue transplants could otherwise save. The problem now isn't the technology or the capability of successful transplantation. The roadblock now is that there simply aren't enough organs to go around.

The Future Fix?

The emerging field of regenerative medicine promises to solve the problem of the organ shortage and transplant rejection by one-day re-growing organs in the lab, using patients' own cells (stem cells, or healthy cells extracted from the donor site.) If you've ever seen the mouse with the ear growing out of his back, you've seen the early evidence of these possibilities. Recently, some of these "bioartificial" organs have already become a reality. For instance, by the end of 2010, 30 patients became the proud owners of the first lab-grown bladders without any significant complications.

The science fiction sounding grown bladders technique was developed by Anthony Atala of the Wake Forest Institute for Regenerative Medicine. Basically speaking, researchers took healthy cells from the patients own diseased bladders, caused them to multiply like crazy, then applied them to a balloon-like scaffold made of collagen. As Atala said, "It's like baking a layer cake. You're layering the cells one layer at a time, spreading these toppings." The bladder-to-be is then incubated until the cells form functioning tissue. Six to eight weeks later, a new disease-free bladder is born and is ready to be swapped out for the old one.

The hope is to be able to someday use a similar process to grow kidneys, livers, and other badly needed organs. Because these organs have so many intricate blood vessels, they present more challenges. Research is currently under way in about a dozen major university and corporate laboratories with the latest incarnations of 3-D printers. Instead of extruding plastic, metal or ceramics, these printers squirt an ink of living cells. These machines can build up the tissue structure layer by layer into virtually any shape, possibly even solving the intricacy issue by printing out tiny tubes suitable for blood vessels.

It's estimated that it may be five years or more before even the simplest of these experimental prototypes is ready for clinical testing. Problems range from the challenge of keeping large tissue structures alive to the lack of computerized tools for personalized organ design. Experts estimate that it won't be until the year 2030 that we will be able to safely grow organs to meet the demand and potentially solve the organ shortage crisis forever.

So what do we do for the next couple of decades for the tens of thousands who will die before science is able to catch up? The only feasible solution is to expand the pool of donors with every willing individual who is healthy enough and capable of giving of their extra or regenerative parts. More donors equal more lives saved.

There are certainly enough people on the planet that can more than compensate for the organ shortage in the world today. Why do we continue to have such a shortage of usable parts? It begins with the development of transplant laws and the regulations set forth by the transplant community.

Organ Transplant Laws

As transplantation became more advanced, both developing and developed countries forged various policies to try to increase the safety and availability of organ transplants for their citizens. Much of this has continued to be trial and error, as no country seems to have been able to successfully supply enough organs to meet the demand for their citizens who need them.

The problem can be emphasized by simply looking at systems used by other countries. For example, there are two primary systems in the world for voluntary donations. There is the "opt-in" system, such as we have in the U.S. wherein you must give explicit consent to be a donor to considered as a donor. Then there is the "opt-out" system, where anyone who has not explicitly refused to donate is automatically considered to be an organ and tissue donor, (also known as the "presumed consent" system.) You would think that we'd be able to simply look at these two systems to determine which is most effective in increasing donor organs and tissue, but this is not the case.

Because of various factors contributing to the rate of transplantations in a country, including the rate of living donors, hospital connectivity, and demand, there is no direct correlation between a countries' chosen system and the rate of donation. Some countries with an opt-out system have what are considered to be relatively high donor rates. Spain, for instance, has 34 donors per million inhabitants. Other countries with the same opt-out system have weak donor rates. Greece, for example, has a rate of only six donors per million. Sweden's rate is in the middle with a rate of 15 donors per million.[1] Therefore, there is no conformity as to which system works best. Because of that, each country is in a constant state of trying to figure out what to try next to increase donor numbers. Unfortunately, there has been no clear consensus.

United States

Under U.S. law, the regulation of organ donation is left to states within the limitations of the federal National Organ Transplant Act

(NOTA) of 1984. However, most states have conformed to the federal Uniform Anatomical Gift Act (UAGA), streamlining the process and standardizing the rules between states. Likewise, most states have made it simple for anyone who would like to donate by encouraging them to state their consent whenever they go in for a driver's license renewal, which is noted directly on their state-issued IDs. Additionally, state-run donor registries communicate with other state registries to allow for a central information center for an individual's wish to be a donor.

The U.S. remains a pure consent system, requiring donors to overtly make their wish to donate known. But even then, there is no guarantee that they will donate once they die, because many states allow for your choice to be overridden by your loved ones who may not like the idea of you being parted out. Without enough volunteers, and the fact that even a registered donor may not be able to donate, there continues to be a shortage of available organs in this country. There has never been a time in the U.S. when there were sufficient amounts of organs to meet the demand.

Europe

The European Union (EU) likewise does not regulate organ donation uniformly; the decision is left to member states. However, unlike the U.S., each member state widely varies in their chosen donor system. As of 2010, a total of 24 European countries had some form of presumed consent (opt-out) system, with the most prominent and "hardest opt-out systems in Spain, Austria and Belgium yielding high donor rates.[2] In most others, including the United Kingdom (UK), organ donation is voluntary and no consent is presumed, similar to the U.S. system. However, the UK has recently discussed whether to switch to an opt-out system in light of the success in other countries and a severe British organ donor shortfall[3] -- hence, the continual flux by most countries to find a better way, as mentioned earlier.

In 2008, the EU parliament overwhelmingly voted for an initiative to introduce an EU organ donor card in order to foster organ donation in Europe, the results of which are, as yet, unclear.

Other Countries

Whilst potential recipients in developing countries may mirror their more developed counterparts in desperation, potential donors in developing countries do not. In addition to the citizens waiting for organ transplants in the U.S. and other developed nations, there are long waiting lists in the rest of the world. More than 2 million people need organ transplants in China, over 60,000 are waiting in Latin America (90% of which are waiting for kidneys), as well as thousands more in the less documented continent of Africa. Donor bases vary widely in developing countries, oftentimes rooted in the beliefs of the individuals in those countries.

For instance, organ donation is Japan has been stymied due to a controversial transplant in 1968 that caused a distrust of western medicine. Because of that, as well as other cultural reasons, the rate of organ donation in Japan is significantly lower than in most Western countries.[4]

Traditions and culture have always presented a challenge to donor numbers in many countries. For example, traditionally Muslims believe body desecration in life or death to be forbidden, and thus many reject organ transplantation.[5] While Muslim authorities nowadays accept the practice if another life will be saved,[6] religious traditions are deep-set and continue to negatively affect donor numbers.

Likewise, there is a severe donor shortage in Israel due to similar religious objections over the desecration of the body. Some Orthodox rabbis oppose organ donations altogether, while others advocate that they participate in all decision-making regarding a particular donor. As a result, only about 10% of Israeli adults hold donor cards, (compared with 30% in Western countries.) Some Israeli organizations, such as the Halachic Organ Donor Society (HODS) are working to increase knowledge and participation in organ donation among Jews throughout the world.[7] In 2010, Israel passed a first-of-its-kind law to encourage more organ donation by allowing donor card holders preference should they need a transplant. However, currently about one-third of all heart transplants performed on Israelis are done abroad in place like the Peoples Republic of China or other parts of Europe.

Even the type of donation varies widely by country. For example, in Uruguay, Cuba and Chile, 90% of organ transplants come from cadaveric donors. Whereas, cadaveric donors only represent 35% of donors in Saudi Arabia. There is continuous effort to increase the utilization of cadaveric donors in Asia, however the popularity of living, single kidney donors in India yields India a strikingly low cadaveric donor prevalence of less than one person per million.

Organ transplantation in China has taken place since the 1960's, and China has one of the largest transplant programs in the world, peaking at over 13,000 transplants a year by 2004.[8] Organ donation, however, is against Chinese tradition and culture[9] and involuntary donation is illegal under Chinese law.[10] As discussed later in-depth, China's transplant program attracted the attention of international news media in the 1990's due to ethical concerns about the organs and tissue removed from the corpses of executed criminals.[11]

Iran is the only country in the world that has claimed to solve its kidney shortage, by unabashedly paying its citizens to "donate." Reports of the exact amount of compensation have varied, but one bioethicist seems to be in the know. Dr. Sigrid Fry-Revere, a bioethicist and founder of Stop Organ Trafficking Now, advocates for the Iranian way, claiming, "Kidney donors receive an average the equivalent of six months' salary for a registered nurse in Iran, or approximately $32,000. All receive at least one year of health insurance and an exemption from Iran's two-year mandatory military service. In many regions of the country there is a waiting list for people who want to donate."[12] If true, this may ultimately be the solution to the kidney shortage. However, due to the world's view of Iran's many human rights violations, it is unlikely that other countries will follow this practice of legalizing the sale of body parts anytime soon.

Whether other countries permit the selling of body parts or not, these sales are already occurring all over the world, with increasing frequency. Because of the organ shortage in every country, as is the case with any high-demand low-supply scenario, there is a booming black market industry of organ sales.

Organ Trafficking and the Law

In 2008, police officers smashed open the doors of a dairy farm in northern India and found 17 people hooked up to IV tubes, being drained of blood, too weak to run away. The farmer and his staff had kept them alive to milk their veins and sell off the contents to local blood banks.[13]

In 2009, authorities in India broke up a ring involving doctors, nurses, paramedics and hospitals that had performed 500 illegal transplants of organs to rich Indians and foreigners. Most of the donors were poor laborers who were paid up to $2,500 for kidneys. Some were reportedly forced to give up organs at gunpoint.

When the Indian government moved victims of the 2004 tsunami into the Tsunami Nagar tent camp in Chennai, illegal organ-brokers flocked to the scene. The camp came to be known as Kidneyville, due to the amount of kidneys that were procured from paid tsunami survivors. Within a year, doctors from 52 Indian hospitals performed 2,000 illegal kidney operations.

The World Health Organization (WHO) estimates that about 10% of the 63,000 kidneys transplanted worldwide each year from living donors have been bought illegally. Lungs, pieces of liver and corneas also command a price. Many countries have difficulty enforcing the illegal trade in their country. However, while some countries, most notably the Indian government, claim to have trouble tracking the flourishing organ black market in their country, they have yet to officially condemn it. Other countries victimized by illegal organ trade have implemented legislative reactions. For example, China made the selling of organs illegal as of July 2006 (claiming that even prisoner organ donors have filed consent – which will be discussed in later chapters.)

Despite these efforts, illegal trafficking continues to thrive. This can, in part, be attributed to the lack of adequate legal organ donations and the corruption in healthcare systems, which have been traced as high up as the doctors themselves in China, Ukraine, and India. The blind-eye economically strained governments and healthcare programs must sometimes turn to organ trafficking, stuck between the proverbial rock and a hard place in wanting their citizens to survive but not having the means to provide organs for them.

Even the United States is not immune. In 2011, a 60-year-old man from Brooklyn, New York pleaded guilty to illegally brokering kidney sales in the U.S. Between 2006 and 2009, he arranged transplants for three New Jersey patients with renal failure. The donors were poor Israelis who were flown to the U.S. for their surgeries, for which the broker was paid about $160,000. But there are many U.S. citizens who have traveled to other countries to likewise receive transplants, whose organs came from questionable suppliers, at best.

One of the driving forces for illegal organ trafficking and for "transplantation tourism" is the price differences for organs and transplant surgeries in different areas of the world. According to the New England Journal of Medicine, a human kidney can be purchased in Manila for $1000 – $2000, but in urban Latin America, a kidney may cost more than $10,000. Kidneys in South Africa have sold for as a high as $20,000. Price disparities based on donor race are a driving force of attractive organ sales in South Africa, as well as in other parts of the world.

In China, a kidney transplant operation runs for around $70,000, liver for $160,000, and heart for $120,000.[14] Although these prices are still unattainable to the poor, compared to the fees of the U.S., where a kidney transplant may demand $100,000, a liver $250,000, and a heart $860,000, bargain Chinese prices have made China a major provider of organs and transplantation surgeries to other countries.

Some governments, under pressure from civil rights and advocacy groups, are beginning to show signs of trying to fight the influx illegally obtained organs. For example, starting on May 1, 2007, doctors involved in commercial trade of organs faced fines and suspensions in China. Additionally, now only a few certified hospitals are allowed to perform organ transplants in order to curb illegal transplants.[15]

Despite the crackdowns of various governments, the black market trade for organs continues to flourish. It's a plain fact of economics, and the reality of what most that are desperate for a working organ will do to save their life or the lives of a loved one. It's no doubt this illegal trade will continue right up until the day that a breakthrough in science arrives or the amount of donors increases sufficiently to accommodate the need.

The Shortage Persists

Although transplant technologies continue to improve, the need for organs continues to outpace the supply all around the world. No government has been able to come up with the answer to definitively solve this problem. The donor pool is simply too small. While some have proposed creative solutions to increase the supply of organs throughout recent decades, most proposals are wrought with dilemmas from ethical roadblocks to government resistance. Until we are literally able to manufacture viable organs, it's likely that this shortage will persist.

There are things that can be done today, however, to increase the pool of healthy donors immediately. It's likely that an increased pool will be able to drastically reduce the numbers of those who die unnecessarily now in this country, if not stem the tide of organ and tissue shortage in the U.S. altogether. The pioneering physicians at the outset of this chapter continued beyond their initial failures to discover ways to save lives. We have a pool of willing healthy donors who are asking the transplant community to give a detailed look at the option of accepting them as a potential solution to the organ shortage crisis in this country.

We'll see that history once held legitimate concerns that required regulations to discourage prisoner organ and tissue donations, despite the decrease in donor numbers. However, we'll also see that despite the passing of decades of technological advances and the evolution of the transplant field, transplant policy-makers have failed to adequately reconsider whether these previous recommendations against use of inmate organs and tissue are still legitimate concerns. Without expanding the donor pool, the shortage of organs and tissue for transplantation will continue to persist in this country. It is, therefore, overdue and necessary to take a new meaningful look at the option of healthy and willing prisoner organ and tissue donors now.

MILESTONES IN SUCCESSFUL ORGAN DONATION AND TRANSPLANTATION

1869 – First "transplant" (Skin graft)
1905 – First cornea transplant
1954 – First kidney transplant (donated by living identical twin)
1962 – First kidney and lung transplants from deceased donors
1967 – First liver transplant
1967 – First heart transplant (S. Africa)
1968 – First heart transplant (U.S.)
1968 – First pancreas transplant
1968 – Uniform Anatomical Gift Act (UAGA) established (made organ and tissue donation legal)
1982 – First combined heart/lung transplant
1983 – FDA approves Cyclosporine (reduces recipients rejection of organs)
1983 – First lung lobe transplant
1984 – First combined heart/liver transplant
1984 – National Organ Transplant Act (NOTA) established (prohibits selling of organs)
1984 – Organ Procurement and Transplantation Network (OPTN) established (fair organ allocation)
1986 – United Network for Organ Sharing (UNOS) established (provides services for OPTN)
1986 – First double lung transplant
1987 – Medicare begins covering heart transplants
1990 – Medicare begins covering liver transplants
1990 – Nobel Prize awarded to pioneers in living kidney and bone marrow transplants
1991 – First small intestine transplant
1995 – First living-donor kidney transplant (laparoscopically)
1998 – First living-donor partial pancreas transplant
1998 – First hand transplant
1999 – First engineered bladder transplant
2003 – April designated as "National Donate Life Month"
2005 – First partial facial transplant
2006 – First jaw transplant (combining donated jaw w/recipients bone marrow)

2006 – Lab-grown bladders were first implanted into children with spina bifida
2008 – First double-arm transplant
2008 – First baby born from transplanted ovary
2008 – First engineered windpipe transplant
2010 – First full facial transplant
2013 – UNOS forced to change lung allocation policy to allow children better placement on adult lists
2013 – Compensation for bone marrow donations made legal

Chapter 2

Organ Donation and Prisoners

There continues to be a never-ending shortage of suitable organs for transplantation in most countries, and the United States is no exception. In the U.S., over 135,000 people are on official waiting lists for organs or bone marrow needed for survival. (Over 121,000 for organs and over 14,000 for bone marrow – as of November 2013[16]) Only about 1 in 7 of those on the waiting list will reach the front of the line and get the organ or tissue they need. That means the other six of those in the organ and tissue line are doomed.

Major organs and tissues that can be transplanted	
Deceased Donor Only	Living or Deceased Donor
Heart	Kidney
Stomach	Lung
Full Pancreas	Partial Pancreas
Full Liver	Liver Lobe
Full Intestine	Partial Intestine
Bladder	Skin
Hand	Islets of Langerhan
Cornea	Blood
Face	Bone Marrow
Blood Vessels	Heart Valve

Additionally, there is another uncounted number who need organs but who are not even able to find a spot in line on official waiting lists due to poor health conditions that make them unlikely candidates to actually survive an organ transplant.

Due to the shortage of available donors and healthy organs, many will die before they have a chance to get the lifesaving part they need. While some may only have to wait for a matter of months to receive a heart, others will have to wait for years to receive the part they need. Of those waiting for organs, three-quarters are waiting for a kidney,[17] due in large part to the prevalence of high blood pressure, obesity and diabetes in society today. As such, kidneys have much longer wait-times and many die while waiting. The demand is that dire, and the supply that sparse.

Every day, on average, eighteen will die while waiting for an organ and another six will die while waiting for a bone marrow transplant. There are certainly enough people in the U.S. who are healthy enough to donate, but there is a shortage of those willing to proactively sign up as organ donors or to actively pursue giving of their organ or tissue to others in need. With the increasing demand for healthy organs and tissue, the numbers of those who will die while waiting in line will continue to increase... unless more donors can be found.

Organ Donors

Each donor body can save up to eight lives with a healthy heart, two lungs, two kidneys, pancreas, and liver (divided in two.) Additionally, one body can provide over 50 other organs and tissues that can used to extend or enhance life for those who need them through transplants of skin, bones, blood, valves, corneas, and many other parts. With that many available parts per human, it doesn't seem like there could be a shortage. But there is, and the shortage increases daily.Organ donors may be living, dead or "brain dead." The ideal

Average Wait-times For Organs	
Heart	230 days
Liver	796 days
Lungs	1068 days

donor, from the transplant communities' perspective, is a brain dead donor because although the donor is technically dead, their body is still functional enough to best preserve the organs until they can be transplanted. Brain dead means the donor must have received an injury (either traumatic or pathological) to the part of the brain that controls heartbeat and breathing. Breathing is maintained via artificial sources, which, in turn, maintains heartbeat. Once brain death has been declared, the person can be considered for organ donation. However, because less than 3% of all deaths in the U.S. are the result of brain death, and due to the fact that most brain dead donors come in the form of accident victims, they are simply too few to make much of a dent in the organ crisis. Therefore, there is a great need for donations from other types of donors, such as organs donated post-mortem and while the donor is still alive.

Organ donations from deceased donors are the most common types of organ donation. If a donor dies in the hospital or is discovered shortly after death, their entire body of organs can potentially be used to save many lives. However, because organs only stay useful within such a short window period after death, there is no guarantee that a dead donor's organs or tissue will be able to be used in time. The retrieval of organs must take place in most cases within a few hours after the body has died, although technologies are improving to be able to preserve organs for up to a day or two under the right conditions.

Unlike organs, however, most tissues can be preserved and stored for years. Tissue may be recovered from those who are cardiac dead. That is, their breathing and heartbeat has ceased. They are referred to as cadaveric donors. In general, tissues may be recovered from donors up to 24 hours past the cessation of heartbeat. In contrast to organs, most tissues (with the exception of corneas) can be preserved and stored for up to five years, meaning they can be "banked". Also, more than 60 grafts may be obtained from a single tissue donor. Because of these three factors, the ability to recover from a non-heart beating donor, the ability to bank tissue and the number of grafts available from each donor, tissue transplants are much more common than organ transplants. The American Association of Tissue Banks estimates that more than one million tissue transplants take place in the United States each year. Living donors present the best option for healthy organ donation. The donor remains alive and donates a renewable tissue, such as blood or bone marrow, or donates an organ, primarily a kidney or a partial donation of a liver. Obviously, because the

HOW LONG ORGANS ARE USEFUL AFTER DEATH	
Heart	6 hours
Kidneys	48–72 hours
Liver	12–24 hours
Lungs	6 hours

living donor also needs organs to survive, they are limited to giving only those parts that regenerate, or that, by nature, we can afford to do without.

Because a donation of a living organ can be scheduled between an already healthy donor and the recipient, the likelihood of a successful transplant is much greater. Likewise, the duration of the donor part is far greater. For example, a kidney donated from a living donor will continue functioning for an average of 15.5 years; a deceased donor kidney will typically only last half as long. Doctors say a live donor even trumps a "perfect match" between a cadaveric donor and recipient.

Those related to the recipient currently make most living donations. Typically, it is easier to find a match because of the genetic similarities between donor and recipient. This helps to ensure a greater probability that the recipient's body will accept the donated organ. However, living donations can easily be made to and from perfect strangers. In the case of kidney donations, for example, if a stranger is the same blood type as the donor, there is a strong likelihood that he is a match for transplantation. Called "altruistic" donations, some donate to whoever is the next person on the waiting list; others use some other method of choosing a recipient based on criteria important to them. If a donor doesn't have an immediate family member or someone they know in need of an organ, this is the type of donation where they could have the greatest impact. Unfortunately, due to insufficient donor numbers, living altruistic donations only account for about 3% of total organ donations.

With limited numbers of close enough matches to keep up with the demand for organs, the Alliance for Paired Donation (APD) was established in 2006. The goal of the APD is to get more kidneys to more people who need them through "paired exchanges." A paired exchange is a technique of matching willing living donors to compatible recipients other than the recipient they wanted to give to, yet guaranteeing that their loved one also receives the needed organ. For example, a husband may be willing to donate a kidney to his wife, but cannot since there isn't a biological match. Another willing spouse may have the same problem of incompatibility with his or her partner. Instead of just living with the fact that they aren't matches, doctors pair up the opposite spouse matches so that both can get the kidneys they need.

To find matches, this may sometimes involve more than just the two couples. It's not uncommon to now find paired exchanges between a web of a dozen patients or more. The first such complex multi-hospital kidney exchange, performed in February 2009, involved 12 patients. It involved a coordinated effort between hospitals all around the country -- the Johns Hopkins Hospital in Baltimore, Barnes-Jewish Hospital in St. Louis and Integris Baptist Medical Center in Oklahoma City.[18] Another 12-patient multi-hospital kidney exchange was performed four weeks later by Saint Barnabas Medial Center in Livingston, New Jersey, Newark Beth Israel Medical Center and New York-Presbyterian Hospital.[19] In December 2009, a 13-organ 13-recipient matched kidney exchange took place, coordinated through Georgetown University Hospital and Washington Hospital Center, Washington DC.[20] Surgical teams led by Johns Hopkins continue to pioneer in this field by having more complex chain of exchange such as a recent record-setting 16-patient, eight-way multihospital kidney exchange.[21] Out of necessity, these paired exchanges are being used more widely.

Health Risks to Living Donors

There are typically very few complications surrounding the health of an otherwise healthy organ donor after the donation procedure. The reason that they are allowed at all is premised on the theory that the donor will not normally suffer long-term harm.

The most common living organ donation is a kidney. Kidney donations are done laparoscopically, removing a kidney through a couple of small incisions; a now common procedure. Only tiny scars remain and the donor usually feels normal again in two to four weeks, while the remaining kidney is growing to compensate. Even under the terrible scenario that a person gets kidney disease in the future, the disease affects both kidneys. Therefore, as far as donation goes, a donor is not giving away his spare. Other risks are infrequent and the risk of a fatality is almost non-existent (currently less than .03% for kidney donors, or 3 in 10,000[22])

Similarly, liver donors typically fare well. The donation consists of a lobectomy, where just a small portion of the liver is excised for transplantation. Because this requires a bigger incision and is thus more invasive, the actual recovery time can be longer and can present additional complications – although complications are exceptionally infrequent. Recovery of the remaining part of the organ is rapid, with little further care necessitated.

Bone marrow donation presents the lowest risk of all transplantation procedures, especially given today's technologies making bone marrow donation similar to blood donation. Fatal complications as of the mid-90's rested at less than 1 in 10,000 at their worst.[23] The number of complications today is insignificant.

There are over 350 million people in the U.S., more than enough to compensate for the 135,000 waiting list for organs and tissue. The procedures for donating living parts like a kidney or bone marrow are relatively simple and without risks when compared to the benefits derived. Recovery is rapid with almost no long-lasting ill effects. By donating, you are saving a life. Why does there continue to be such a shortage of organs and tissue in the U.S.?

The Challenge

Transplantation medicine is one of the most challenging and complex areas of modern medicine. Transplantation and donation both raise all sorts of difficult-to-navigate concerns. Take bioethical issues, for example. These include the definition of death, when and how consent should be given for an organ to be donated and/or transplanted and the payment for organs for transplantation.[24] Or take the ethical issues, including transplantation tourism and more broadly the context in which organ harvesting or transplantation may occur. Still other ethical issues surround who can appropriately even be considered for organ donation, based on social criteria such as prisoners or gays who present a degree of risk. Then let's not forget that a donor has to be healthy enough to donate in the first place.

In the U.S., the United Network for Organ Sharing (UNOS) is in charge. They regulate all things organ transplantation in this country.[25] The U.S. Food and Drug Administration (FDA) regulate the tissue transplant side of things. Together, with input from various public health agencies around the U.S., such as the CDC, they set strict regulations on the safety of the transplants, primarily aimed at the prevention of the spread of communicable disease, but also the overall safety of the donor and recipient alike.

For instance, to ensure that a living kidney donor will fare well after donating one of their kidneys, UNOS sets criteria that the donor must meet prior to the donation. The basics required to donate a kidney include willingness to undergo major surgery, ability to give informed consent, presence of two normal kidneys and general good health. The donor must not only be able withstand the surgery, but also to recover quickly and return to normal activities of daily living. More specifically though, the donor generally cannot be a diabetic, have a body mass index over 35, have high blood pressure, have used any hard drugs within the past two years, (or marijuana within six months), or have any health problems of note, such as cancers or infectious diseases.

These are all very reasonable requirements. But therein lays the challenge for the transplant community and those who need organs. For example, it's estimated that more than a third of all Americans are classified as obese, or as having a BMI over 35. Therefore, right off the top a huge chunk of Americans cannot donate. Add those with high blood pressure, diabetes and prior drug users, and the pool of potential donors thins even more. This is just to protect the donor.

When it comes to protecting the recipient, the transplant policy-makers set equally specific donor criteria. For example, due to high-risk factors and the prior inability of the transplant doctors to guarantee that a disease or infection was not being passed from donor to recipient, the transplant community rejects donors who are gay males, hemophiliacs, and our the topic of this book, all who are incarcerated, amongst others. The donor pool continues to shrink with regulations and safeguards.

From an outside view, it seems that these safeguards must be well founded and sound. They wouldn't be in place otherwise, right? That's especially so, considering the dire need for organs in this country.

The reality is that every regulation set forth by the transplant community must have been decided on for the benefit of all involved... at some point. The problem arises, however, as we'll see later, when the transplant community is quick to enact a policy to protect the overall pool of recipients and donors, but they are slow to evolve with advancements in medical and transplant technologies and ethical climate changes. It's understandable that the policy-makers would not want to be too quick to change standards before the "kinks" have been fully worked out of whatever new development comes on the scene – even when it appears that those developments could save many lives. Nevertheless, there comes a point when the failure to evolve has been delayed far beyond what is rational, to a point of unnecessarily and negligently costing lives.

Prisoners as Donors

The transplant community and policy-makers would like nothing more than to find organs for everyone in need. But they are squeamish about using even willing prisoners to satisfy this need. For reasons that we'll delve into with detail, prisoners have been effectively banned from donating organs, blood and all other tissue since the early 90's.

Ironically, throughout the 60's, 70's and 80's, prisons were considered a great place to hold blood donor drives. Literally, in some places, the equivalent of the bloodmobile would pull up in front of the prison and the inmates would line up to donate. Parole considerations were given for some who chose to donate blood. "Good time" was given as an incentive, and in some cases, inmates were directly paid for their blood donations in the same way that non-prisoner blood donors are compensated today. In the early 90's, that stopped.

Due to the prevalence of AIDS and the difficulties with detection of the relatively new scary virus throughout the late 80's and early 90's, the FDA and the CDC both reasonably issued recommendations against organ and tissue donations from prisoners and other high-risk groups that effectively banned all such donations from prisoners from that point on. Prisons, for reasons we'll discuss, were now considered to be too much of a high-risk environment to accept blood, organs or other tissue from. Since then, organ and tissue donations have not been generally accepted.

No one would rationally argue against such an abrupt change in policy back then. The AIDS scare was very real, and if there was any question as to the capability of appropriately screening potential donors, the only real solution could be to forbid them from the donor pool at all. To allow otherwise would be criminal. But additionally, while making the recommendations against inmate donors, the medical community decided to outline other reasons why it may not be advisable to accept organs and tissue from those trapped in the prison environment. Those recommendations have not changed.

To ask the transplant policy-makers why organ and tissue donations are not widely accepted today from either general population prisoners or death row inmates, you'll receive a statement that looks something (or exactly) like this:

--

"Much concern regarding organ donation by inmates is related to their high risk of exposure to communicable infectious diseases during incarceration, e.g. HIV and various forms of hepatitis. While the availability of better tests for infectious diseases has improved the safety and supply of donated organs, tissue, marrow, and blood, no test is 100% accurate; consequently there is a small percentage of false negative results (meaning an individual actually has the infection, but the test result is negative.

The OPTN/UNOS Ethics Committee has also deliberated on many issues related to organ donations from incarcerated individuals, including: assuring appropriate informed consent for both donors and recipients; the ethical issues of the act of organ donation itself; the uneven application of the death sentence among socio-economic and ethnic groups in many States; and the overall effect of such policies on organ donation in general.

Based on these deliberations, the Committee is opposed to any strategy or proposed statute that would facilitate organ donation from prisoners, condemned or otherwise. It is my opinion that the Committee's position is unlikely to change unless all of these issues can be satisfactorily addressed."

--

That was the thorough, verbatim response that I received from a public health analyst at the U.S. Department of Health and Human Services shortly after my request for information in 2009, answering why the transplant community didn't want my healthy organs or tissue.

Looking at those statements, it is clear that the heads of the transplant community have no interest in accepting inmate donors into the pool of healthy options today. They sound as though they've considered inmate donors throughout recent history, but decided to exclude them for the same reasons they instituted the effective ban decades ago. To read their statements, these reasons seem well thought out, logical and articulated convincingly enough to frighten away anyone contemplating the notion of allowing organ or tissue donation from an incarcerated person. It's no wonder why the prison systems won't generally consider it. They are given an out on a platter.

However, those statements above echo back to the early 90's, and have not changed much despite modern realities. A logical look will find these statements are now outdated at best and, as such, are not universally held within the transplant community, or amongst all transplant professionals.

Many transplant professionals, from transplant surgeons to ethics professors, are in agreement with us that healthy willing prisoners should now be considered for organ and tissue donation. There are reasons for that, which gives us reason to keep pursuing this option. Besides, even the quoted public health analyst left the door cracked. "It is my opinion that the Committee's position is unlikely to change unless all of these issues can be satisfactorily addressed." Sounds like a challenge worth taking up.

Why Would a Prisoner Want to Donate?

Philosophers have debated forever whether a truly selfless altruist even exists. Some say they do – the transplant community is a big believer. Others proclaim, "Scratch an altruist and a hypocrite bleed." When it comes to prisoners, the term "altruist" is certainly not one of the first adjectives that come to mind. In fact, there are more likely thousands of antonyms that would be used long before someone equated 'prisoner' with 'selfless.' So it brings up the question, why would an inmate, who has violated society on such a level that they must be locked up, have any interest in giving up a part of their own body for the benefit of someone they don't know? Many fear that there must be something more to it, some conman's ulterior motive.

My fellow inmates may not appreciate this analogy, but for the purpose of this discussion, you might compare the thought of inmate altruism to monkeys who spend hours on end sitting around all day. You've seen them, contently picking through each other's fur. For monkeys, that act of grooming is the calming social glue that cements relationships within their troop. It lowers the heart rate and tends to lower the stress hormone levels. It brings to mind the 'you scratch my back, I scratch yours,' we are both happier line of thinking.

However, to more closely compare things to what we're discussing, we have to go to a study out of London's Roehampton University of the Barbary macaque monkeys, where Dr. Stuart Semple and his colleagues determined that it wasn't the monkeys who were groomed constantly that had the lower stress hormone levels. Monkeys that were actually doing the grooming the most were the ones that were benefited with these lower levels. Research of other monkey species, as well, proved that it was, in fact, the groomer, not the groomed that enjoyed the decreased behavioral markers of anxiety. It seems to lend credence to the philosophy that it truly is better to give than receive, which was, incidentally, the title of Dr. Semple's research paper.

Not that we're sitting around picking through each other's fur, but maybe it's as simple as the concept with a monkey. We are less stressed when we give than when we receive. Emerging science contends that do-gooding is simply hard-wired into most everyone's brain, free-man and some prisoners alike. According to neuroscientist Donald W. Pfaff, Ph.D., specific brain signals force us to consider our actions as if they were directed at ourselves.[26] "Do unto others as you would have them do unto you," may not have just been Christly advice, but also part of our circuitry. Considering the life of a prisoner who has plenty of time to pay attention to the body's signals, perhaps we just notice the need to do something for someone.

Despite being supposedly hardened criminals, spend a moment as a fly on the wall and you'll hear killers and thieves discuss how they wish they could help the plight of groups in need on some daytime talk show they were watching. Extreme Home Makeover and Ellen or Oprah giveaways are popular shows here. Many prisoners gain the same internal choke-up feelings as the average person sitting home in their living rooms. Just because they violated society once, or even a dozen times, doesn't mean that the parts that do good are missing altogether. Every prison has community outreach programs that help fund society efforts. Whether it's the local little league, domestic violence shelter, or an area Mission, inmates groups - even in the hardest maximum-security settings -- are constantly doing what they can to help benefit others besides themselves. While violations they've committed against society and the subsequent imprisonment may define prisoners in the eyes of the public, these do not necessarily define the inmates in their own eyes.

But to ask an inmate why they want to donate, after you get beyond the generic, "It's the right thing to do," you get a surprisingly varied set of answers -- but with one common theme. Some express that they had an aunt, uncle, niece, or other relatives die while on waiting lists and they just want to honor and respect them. Others want to "pay back society" to compensate for the social norms they've violated. Some wish to do so out a spiritual hope of redemption, to somehow correct their wrongs, or at least take the sharp edges off them. Some feel that it's just logic. It's math. I have something that I don't need, or in the case of my death, a whole body that's otherwise going to waste. What good is it doing in the ground?

Maybe it's a realization after years in a box with limited prospects, resources, or the ability to truly influence somebody else's life in a positive way, that we come equipped, no matter what we've done in other areas of our life, with the means to actually do something more meaningful with our life. Perhaps some hope to donate for reasons less than altruism, for instance, to be seen by the ones they care about, their mothers, or former best friends, as something other than a lost cause of a criminal. We can actually save lives. No matter how hardened you are, there is always somebody that you care about enough that you would do anything in your power to help. Even the worst sort of criminal thinks about that one person. Even if you can't directly do something for that special someone, that loved one becomes your motivation to do something right, if for nothing else than out of love and honor for them.

Whatever the reason, tens of thousands of inmates have in common that they want to give of themselves in this way, saving a life through organ or tissue donation. If we are healthy enough, and we're not in some way materially compensated for it, if it is truly a gift, what does it matter what our reasons are. The fact is that prisoners want to be organ and tissue donors and lives can be saved that are otherwise dying right now.

It is clear that there is a dire need for organs in the U.S. and around the world. It is also apparent that the field of organ transplantation is a complex one where careful consideration must be given to every proposal designed to increase organ donations. It is vital, therefore, that we take a practical and meaningful look into any avenue that increases supply while maintaining the rights of all involved. This includes the proposal to allow voluntary prisoners, as well as other healthy willing groups that are currently overlooked, the right to donate healthy organs to those who will otherwise die without them, as long as safeguards are in place to prevent abuses.

As we'll demonstrate, this is possible right now, and there are far more prisoners than you might have imagined who want to give in this way. If allowed, they will have a tremendous impact in reducing the overall organ shortage in this country.

PART ONE

Prisoners vs. Everyone Else

_____

_____

_____

Prisoners make up over 2 million of the U.S. adult population, a large city worth of people. Even though prisons have stopped being a place for rehabilitation in the U.S., there is a large population of prisoners who would like to do something positive from their circumstances. Many prisoners are involved in community outreach programs that serve to give back to the communities they took from. Others try to better themselves through education or religion. Many simply choose to live out their sentences as peaceably as possible, wishing no harm to anyone. A surprising number, however, would like the opportunity to be able to save lives through organ and tissue donation.

Regardless of the offense that landed them in prison, many are not lifelong criminals by nature. If they had it to do all over again, they would not reoffend. They care about those they left behind. They are genuinely concerned about those they victimized. Many times, they are victims of their own circumstances themselves. Had they been better educated beforehand or had some assistance at the right time, things would have been different. But they are not hardened criminals; they just live around some of them.

Therein lay some of the reasons the transplant community and prisons are reluctant to allow organ donations from prisoners. If someone is in prison, they must be a criminal. If they are criminals, they cannot care about anyone but themselves. If they cannot care about anyone but themselves, their motives must be questioned. If they do not have the "proper" motivation to be an organ donor, then their donation is ethically sullied, which is unacceptable.

Even if the prisoner is truly altruistic, how can you be sure? They live around hardened criminals who spend all day plotting and scheming how to take advantage of others. How do you know that the "willing" donor isn't being pressured into donating for the benefit of some con's family member in need (or for that matter, a prison officials?) How do you know that the donor himself isn't really just a scam-artist seeking some unlawful advantage?

Even if it is proven that the inmate donor sincerely wants to give for the appropriate reasons, they live in the cellar of society- a cesspool of disease and infection. What recipient would want to risk it? How can the transplant community warrant such a risk?

At a casual glance, it appears that allowing organ donations from prisoners would be too dangerous to consider. However, a deeper look brings clarity to the realities of prisoners versus the rest of society and the possibilities of changing the antiquated ban on prisoner organ donation. With an entire city worth of people who could dramatically affect the organ shortage in this country effectively banned from organ donation, it is certainly worth taking that closer look.

DO PRISONERS EVEN WANT TO BE DONORS?

_____

_____

_____

FACTS:

18

THE PERCENTAGE OF THE INMATE POPULATION IN UTAH THAT HAS ALREADY SIGNED UP TO BE ORGAN DONORS SINCE THEIR PRISONER ORGAN DONATION LAW CAME INTO EFFECT.

(6 MONTHS AFTER LAW ENACTED)

14,124

THE NUMBER OF INMATES WHO HAVE SIGNED UP TO BE ORGAN DONORS SINCE 2007 IN ONE ARIZONA COUNTY ALONE – ALL OF WHOM WILL LIKELY NOT BE ALLOWED TO ACTUALLY DONATE IF CURRENT PRISON AND TRANSPLANT POLICY REMAINS HOW IT IS TODAY.

(AS OF 1/28/2013)

52

THE PERCENTAGE OF U.S. DEATH ROW PRISONERS WHO WOULD LIKE TO HAVE THE OPTION OF ORGAN DONATION AFTER EXECUTION.

CHAPTER 3

Prisoners are Disgusting

"NO OTHER INSTITUTION IN THIS SOCIETY HAS A HIGHER CONCENTRATION OF PEOPLE AT SUBSTANTIAL RISK OF HIV INFECTION."

–THE NATIONAL COMMISSION ON ACQUIRED IMMUNE DEFICIENCY SYNDROME (1990 STATEMENT CONCERNING PRISONS.)[27]

The prison lifestyle is disgusting.

Prisoners will turn a few sewing needles and a tape deck motor into a tattoo gun and repeatedly stab hepatitis and AIDS infected flesh, staining the contraption with virus before carrying it to the next guy. Sure, the inmate got the Viking war implement that he wanted inked into his body forever. Meanwhile his skin has just been punctured over and over to soak up the viral goo leftover from the last guy. It's a great way to express pride in your heritage while inviting a mortal enemy into your bloodline.

Everyone knows that prisoners love prison love. Nobody beyond a prison wall wants to imagine what takes place in the showers in the pokey, yet "Don't drop the soap" has become the number one prison tip to live by thanks to the stereotype. The ratio of men to women in a prison is hundreds to one, and that "1" is a prison cop. A man without a willing woman for miles (and years) around make for a very pained man. Some choose to cure that pain with homosexual intercourse.

The most common way of transmitting HIV and Hepatitis C in the real world is through male-to-male sexual contact. A close second is by intravenous drug use and sharing needles. When the large majority of the prison population is there for drug-related offenses, it is a virtual guarantee that an inmate will spend a good portion of his day trying to figure out how to get a fix. If you want to see which prisoners those might be, look down a prison tier when a diabetic is getting a shot of insulin. They'll be the ones with their faces pressed against the bars or with their mirrors poked out for a view. If one could get their hands on a needle and some junk, a few dozen guys could be highly entertained for a few hours. You can get the junk, but it's not as though they sell needles on prison canteens and it's not like there is any sterilizing rubbing alcohol around (or someone would drink it). For every needle user in prison there is a man courting a killer virus.

One electric razor may be used by a cellblock of 100 unsavory neighbors.

A friend may be enjoying a spread of sausages, beans, cheeses, and ramen noodles and send some down to the next guy to be neighborly. However, it was the guy a few cells away, the one who didn't know he had hepatitis C, who did the chopping and cooking.

You could go to patch a hole in your prison blues with the sewing needle another guy just accidentally punctured his hepatitis-infested fingertip with as he was patching his own jeans.

You are now infected with hepatitis C and you don't even know it.

Prison is a society with its own forced cultural habits and norms, and many of those "norms" are not exactly clean or healthy. Prison seems like a viral minefield. From the sound of it, most prisoners are as bad off as those on organ donor lists are, or they are on their way to needing organ transplants themselves. Who in their right mind would ever accept an organ donation from such a dangerous and disgusting place? Is it even feasible to use willing inmate donors to increase the donor pool and help with the shortage of available organs?

To answer those questions, it is important to get knee-deep into HIV and hepatitis. We really need to understand just how prevalent these diseases are in prison compared with the rest of the world. Most vital to the conversation, however, we must know how these virus' are detected and if they can be successfully screened out before they infect someone who is already dying from their own terrible disease.

The Facts?

First off, the prison lifestyle isn't quite that universally disgusting, but that is the public perception, thanks to television and Hollywood horror stories. Nevertheless, it is absolutely a high-risk environment for infectious diseases. However, it is not so bad as to count out the possibility of prisoner organ donations. But those who disapprove of prisoner organ donations will quickly display the above stereotype as a potent scare tactic to dissuade from its use. So what are the facts?

A study conducted in the early 90's by the National Institute of Justice showed that the incidence rate of those who were reported to have AIDS was one out of every 495 prisoners in federal and state correction facilities. That was in comparison to 1 in 6,826 in the general public.[28] Prisoners were reportedly infected with AIDS about 13 times more per capita than the rest of the U.S. population. A concerning figure, for sure.

Because of the prevalence of HIV, in the early 90s the Centers for Disease Control and Prevention (CDC) recommended that inmates be completely excluded from organ donations.[29] One year later, the Food and Drug Administration (FDA) advised blood and plasma clinics not to accept any blood donations from prison inmates.[30] The inability to screen such donations effectively enough to guarantee that no prisoner would infect the public far outweighed the need for blood products in the U.S. Remember, the discussions of AIDS at that time were fresh and scary enough on their own. Mix the prevalence of that disease in the prison environment with conversations about taking a piece from a prisoner to make someone else healthier would not exactly exude confidence in the transplant community.

But this was the early 1990s. These references are now over two decades old. Yet, these are the reports that those opposed to organ donations by inmates continue to rely on to prevent willing prisoner donations today.

Are these views still valid?

With the increased awareness of HIV/AIDS and other diseases, as well as the technological advances of modern day testing and organ transplant science, is it possible that these concerns might today be muted?

Given the increased need for organs in the U.S, should organ donations by willing prisoners now be reconsidered?

Let's start by considering these questions and take a deeper, more modern look into to the high-risk comparisons between today's prisoners and the rest of U.S. society.

Inmates vs. the Rest of the United States

Admittedly, prisoners are at high risk for infectious disease. The prison lifestyle is not saintly. There is drug abuse and dirty needle usage, dangerous sexual habits, and other unclean practices. Therefore, there continues to be much concern over the transmission of AIDS and other diseases. Moreover, because prisoners often hail from segments of society that are considered to be at "high risk" in the first place, the possibility for infectious disease is a very real concern to have.

The studies in the early 90's clearly demonstrated the dangers and the disparity between prisons and the rest of the country at that time. But have those numbers remained consistent?

It was as recently as 2009 that the Public Health Analyst from the U.S. Department of Health and Human Services responded to my inquiries regarding continuing dilemmas and concerns over inmate donors, stating in part:

"Much concern regarding organ donation by inmates is related to their high risk of exposure to communicable infectious diseases during incarceration, e.g. HIV and various forms of hepatitis. While the availability of better tests for infectious diseases has improved the safety of the supply of donated organs, tissues, marrow, and blood, no test is 100% accurate..."

If those reasons continue to be used today by public health analysts for transplant community, it would seem that those same early 90s concerns continue to exist today. Over two decades later, is this still the case? There's no better place to find answers than to look at the stats from the prison system itself.

The U.S Department of Justice through their Bureau of Justice Statistics (BJS) is the go-to place for reports on the rates of disease prevalence in U.S. prisons. The most detailed reports on disease prevalence in U.S. prisons concern the spread of HIV and AIDS. By examining this report, we are provided with the best barometer for measuring the spread of infectious disease in prisons over the years.

The latest report (2007–08) showed that out of 1.6 million state and federal prisoners in the U.S., (excluding local and county jails), 21,987 were reported to be HIV positive or to have confirmed AIDS, or about 1.4% of the prison population. Looking at how this

60   LETHAL REJECTION

compares to recent years, this number has remained relatively

	Total **combined** HIV/ AIDS cases in prison			Percentage of prisoners infected		
	2006	2007	2008	2006	2007	2008
Reported	21,985	21,666	21,987	1.7%	1.5%	1.4%

stable.

The BJS report then lays out for us how the rate of infection for AIDS compares with the rest of the U.S. It reveals that in 2007, prisoners accounted for nearly 2½ times more known AIDS infections than the U.S. general population. However, this number decreased to nearly 1½ a year later. (Remember, these are confirmed AIDS diagnoses. The numbers are much different when combined with HIV figures, which we'll discuss in a minute.)

	Percent of population estimated to have confirmed AIDS		Ratio of AIDS cases in prisons to cases in U.S. population
	Prisoners	U.S. Population	
2007	0.41	0.17	2.4
2008	0.36	0.19	1.7

While those numbers are scary, they are far less than what the National Institute of Justice reported in the early 90s. Remember, they stated that the number of prisoners with AIDS was <u>13 times</u> more prevalent than in non-prisoners.

The gap in the infection rates of prisoners versus the U.S. general population has drastically and steadily declined year over year. Yet, when we say that prisoners are almost twice as likely (1.7%) to be infected with AIDS than the rest of the country, that disparity between infection rates of prisons and the U.S. population still seems very significant. But is it? One important aspect of assuring the accuracy in statistical data is ensuring that you are comparing apples to apples. The statistics cited thus far are misleading in that regard. Not to confuse with technicalities, but we're trying to determine exactly how much more high-risk prisoners are than the rest of the world. Accuracy is important, so please bear with me for a second.

Prisoners vs. U.S. population A History ----- How much more prevalent has AIDS been in prison than in the rest of the country?	
1992	13.3 times greater
2002	3.2
2003	3.1
2004	3.1
2005	2.7
2006	2.7
2007	2.4
2008	1.7

Prisoners are people age 18 and older. However, the figures the BJS uses to compare the U.S. population prevalence to prisoners are derived from data that measure U.S. population groups that are 15 and older, and sometimes 13 and older.[31] The number comparisons aren't exactly apples to apples. Those three to five years may not sound concerning, but they lend to some much-skewed ratios.

This is not necessarily due to any bias on the part of the BJS statisticians. The source of their data for the U.S. population AIDS prevalence stems from the CDC's HIV Surveillance Reports. These reports only supply data age-ranges of 15-19 and then from the 20-24 age range. Since prisoners are aged 18 and up, for the sake of accurate numbers when comparing the prison population to the rest of the U.S., the statisticians really needed to be able to have the data broken down a step further to include the 18–24 age range. But no such range existed in the CDC's reports and therefore that range could not be used in the BJS methodology. Instead, statisticians are forced either to add 3 years to the U.S. population, age 15–19, data, or to subtract 2 years from the prison, age 20–24, data to get to that age 18 starting point.

I know, this sounds a little confusing and unimportant. The bottom line, though, is that no matter how you cut it, the numbers showing the prevalence of AIDS in prison compared with those in the rest of the U.S. population are not exactly perfect. Basically, it's this: To get the number they got, the BJS number crunchers used the data from the widest pool available to them - the 15 to 24-age range. If they used their other choice of data -- from the 20 and older range -- suddenly, the ratio of AIDS between prisoners and the rest of the U.S. shrinks from 2.4 to 1.9 for 2007 and to 1.4 for 2008. So the true numbers are somewhere in between. It is probably more accurate to say that prisoners are closer to 1½ times more likely to have AIDS than those in the general U.S. population.

The intent, though, is not to minimize the actual numbers of prisoners with AIDS diagnoses. The intent is to simply be as accurate as possible in determining how much more concerning are prisoners than the rest of the world when it comes to considering the use of their organs or tissue for transplants. There is no doubt that prisoners, in fact, do fit the "high risk" category. But there are degrees of risk that deserve a closer look.

"No other institution…has a higher concentration of people at substantial risk of HIV infection."

We've already seen that we cannot just look at numbers and trust that they tell the whole story. Comparing concentrated prison populations to the much more diverse and varied populations of the United States when it comes to health is like trying to compare fish in a barrel to an ocean of fish. When a society is forced to live in such close proximity, especially given certain sociological and behavioral makeup, the numbers will always appear drastic and concerning over more sparse populations. The numbers are not realistic representations of the issue.

Therefore, it is important to compare like populations. AIDS is primarily an urban disease. The majority of individuals diagnosed with AIDS reside in areas with more than 500,000 people. Areas hardest hit include Miami and Jacksonville, Florida; New Orleans and Baton Rouge, Louisiana; New York City; Baltimore, Maryland; Washington D.C.; and San Francisco, California. Since the prison system is essentially one big city, we have to compare these metropolitan/urban populations to gain a more realistic and thorough view of the differences between prisoners and the rest of U.S. society. Fortunately, the government provides those numbers. Here is what they reveal:

Greatest Risk for HIV/AIDS (Combined):

The following comparison of prisoners to other high-risk populations shows that prisoners while "high-risk" do not present the greatest risk for combined HIV/AIDS infections as previously believed. (Figures are from 2007 CDC & BJS reports)

Areas of higher risk than the prison populations are shaded

	HIV/AIDS Combined		
Prisoners	1 in 72		
U.S. Population	1 in 180		Greater Risk Over Prison
African American			
• Ages 20–54	1 in 40		+1.8x
• Florida	1 in 28		+2.6x
• New Jersey	1 in 28		+2.6x
• New York	1 in 23		+3.1x
Hispanic/Latino	1 in 117		
• Ages 20–54	1 in 98		
• Florida	1 in 98		
• Connecticut	1 in 46		+1.6x
• New York	1 in 35		+2.0x
All Races			
• Males	1 in 118		
• Florida	1 in 96		
• New York	1 in 71		+1.0x
Metropolitan Areas			
• Miami, Florida	1 in 55		+1.3x
• New York, NY	1 in 58		+1.2x

	AIDS Only 2007		
Prisoners	1 in 274		
U.S. Population	1 in 656		Greater Risk Over Prison
African American			
• Washington DC	1 in 34		+8.1x
Hispanic/Latino			
• Pennsylvania	1 in 151		+1.8x
• Washington DC	1 in 75		+3.6x
All Races			
• Washington DC	1 in 52		+6.0x

• Maryland	1 in 260	+1.1x
Metropolitan Areas		
• San Francisco	1 in 146	+1.9x
• Washington DC	1 in 243	+1.1x

"High Risk" Donors Accepted!

Prisoners are a high-risk population. No argument there. The numbers still show that prisoners are about 1½ times more likely to be infected than the U.S. population overall. However, it is evident that HIV and other diseases disproportionately affect certain populations. Those metropolitan areas we mentioned earlier actually all have higher rates of infected than the prison population.

The urban center of Washington D.C. itself has an AIDS prevalence rate that is six times greater than that in prisons. African Americans represent the group most affected, accounting for approximately 12% of the U.S. population but almost half of all new HIV infections. The African American population of prison-aged men has 1½ times more HIV/AIDS infected than do prisons.

It is clear that regardless of race, many U.S. population centers are more HIV/AIDS infected than prisons. Prisoners are a high-risk group, but they are not even close to being the greatest risk.

To follow the same reasoning that the transplant community expresses to reject organ donation from prisoners, the transplant community would likewise disallow organ donations from the entire populations of many U.S. cities, and especially from all African Americans. On the contrary, many of these populations are actually regions of focus for the transplant community to increase organ donations within these areas.

One look at the grants awarded by the U.S. governments' organ donation policy-setters, the Organ Procurement and Transplantation Network (OPTN) and the United Network for Organ Sharing (UNOS), and the double standard between prisons and other "high risk" pools become evident.[32]

One such grant, awarded to the University of Miami Organ Procurement Organization, had a stated purpose to "increase the number of minority organ and tissue donors by increasing intent to donate coupled with family notification of intent to donate among Blacks, Haitians, and Hispanics living in Miami-Dade County, Florida." Miami's HIV/AIDS rate was nearly 1½ times that of prisons, and that is among all races. The minority HIV/AIDS prevalence rate there is well over twice the rate of prisons. The transplant community wants more donors there, is actively seeking more donors from the minorities in this area -- yet inmates are considered to be too high risk?

Even more pointedly, the transplant community has come up with ideas on how to utilize greater risk populations for donations. They've actually recently begun accepting some high-risk donors that they categorize as "expanded-criteria organs" amongst populations with various "behavioral and social risks".[33] It has been reported that an example of those included in this category are deceased IV drug abusers. Additionally, the donation community already transplants organs between donors and patients who are known to be infected with hepatitis C, and there is some consideration under way to do the same for patients infected with HIV patients.[34,35]

At the University of Maryland's School of Medicine, five patients recently received transplants of kidneys that already had cancerous masses on them. When asked why anyone would risk cancer, the Head Surgeon explained, "The ongoing shortage of organs from deceased donors, and the high risk of dying while waiting for a transplant, prompted five donors and recipients to push ahead for surgery." The times are that dire for organs in the U.S.

Expanded-criteria and diseased organs -- and donations from like-infected individuals -- are helping to fill that gap in the shortage of organs in the U.S., but needlessly. The fact that the transplant community has begun accepting those whom they deem as being in an even higher risk category than prisoners signifies the importance of now considering inmate anatomical gifts that are proven to be far safer than some of current options being used or considered. Furthermore, when it comes to death row donors, they are secluded from the rest of the high-risk prison population and are far less likely to contract an infectious disease. For that reason, combined with the advanced notice date of their death, some have gone so far as to refer to death row donors as "super donors."

If organ donations from these populations that show a higher prevalence -- and thus risk for the spread of infectious disease -- than prisons are acceptable to the transplant community, there should be no reason to continue preventing healthy willing inmates from becoming organ donors. Walk into any dialysis clinic or leukemia ward right now in the U.S. and ask a dying patient if they would accept the organs they needed from someone who lives in the high-risk environment of prison, they will invariably say, "absolutely", so long as the organs or tissue were given willingly and the donor is healthy.

However, therein lays the next issue. How can we be certain that the donor is healthy enough to donate? Logic says to simply test them. But it's supposedly not that simple. Remember the contention of the earlier mentioned public health analyst, concerning ensuring that the donors are properly tested? They stated, "no test is 100% accurate." So, how can we be "100%" certain that the donor is healthy?

The nature of the testing for AIDS and hepatitis infections has been such that you could not know for a certainty if a donor was infected at the time of donation. Of course that is a concerning thought. If the donor happens to be coming from a high-risk environment, that concern is even more heightened. When it comes to the high-risk nature of prisons, shouldn't that alone make us think twice about prisoner donations?

TESTS FOR INFECTIOUS DISEASE AREN'T ALWAYS RELIABLE.

_____

_____

_____

FACTS:

1991

THE YEAR PRISONERS WERE BANNED FROM DONATING ORGANS DUE TO INADEQUATE TESTING FOR HIV AND OTHER DISEASES.

6 MONTHS

THE WINDOW PERIOD BETWEEN DISEASE TRANSMISSION AND DETECTION OF THE DISEASE.

(1991)

– – – – – – – – –

2001

THE YEAR APPROPRIATE TESTING FOR HIV INFECTION WAS INTRODUCED IN THE U.S.

5 DAYS

THE CURRENT WINDOW PERIOD BETWEEN DISEASE TRANSMISSION AND DETECTION OF THE DISEASE.

(TODAY)

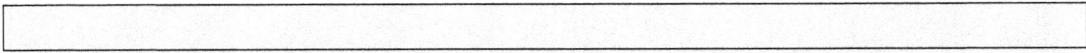

CHAPTER 4

Testing Prisoners for Infectious Disease

"MUCH CONCERN REGARDING ORGAN DONATION BY INMATES IS RELATED TO THEIR HIGH RISK OF EXPOSURE TO COMMUNICABLE INFECTIOUS DISEASES DURING INCARCERATION, E.G. HIV AND VARIOUS FORMS OF HEPATITIS. WHILE THE AVAILABILITY OF BETTER TESTS FOR INFECTIOUS DISEASES HAS IMPROVED THE SAFETY OF THE SUPPLY OF DONATED ORGANS, TISSUE, MARROW AND BLOOD, NO TEST IS 100% ACCURATE..."

–PUBLIC HEALTH ANALYST
FROM THE U.S. DEPARTMENT OF HEALTH AND HUMAN SERVICES (DHHS)

Infections, by nature, are tricky. They show up for war and they intend to win. They're so good at it that detection can be even trickier. Take Hepatitis C for example. Hepatitis C is the inflammation of the liver due to a virus obviously named the hepatitis C virus (HCV). It is the most common cause of the nastiest of liver disorders, such as cirrhosis and liver cancer. About 3.2 million Americans (about 2% of the U.S. population) are estimated to have it, with another estimated 72,000 who will become infected annually.

Making the problem far worse, relatively few people even know they're infected - likely, less than half have any clue that they have the disease. Because of that, it's known as the "silent epidemic." It's not one of the disorders where the infected wake up one morning looking gaunt and emaciated, with telltale signs that they have something wrong with them. You're not bleeding out of places you shouldn't. You don't get the abnormally deep pains in places to tell you something's amiss, like with an inflamed appendix. The virus does very well at masking the fact that it's even there. In fact, because it can take a few decades to do its damage, without a specific test to look for it, you might never know it's there until it's too late. Moreover, even with what the industry has regarded as the appropriate test, the virus seems to play a great game of hide'n'seek for its first few months of life, and may not even be detectable for several months after you're infected.

There are some vague signs of its existence if you're paying attention. Some report symptoms of mild fatigue or generalized weakness, while others complain of a decrease in appetite, some weight loss or depression. However, try looking up those symptoms on your favorite family health guide and you'll find yourself at the beginning of just about any illness from indigestion to the plague. Since we're talking about prisoners here, those symptoms pretty much describe every prison inmate at one time or another.

The medical stat is that only about 25 percent of those with hepatitis experience any symptoms at all. Therefore, most are completely caught off guard when their doctor gives them the diagnosis that they have the virus. When considering this in relation to prison inmates, the fact remains that prisoners are not exactly the most health conscious people on the planet. This is made worse by the fact that even going to the doctor when something is obviously wrong with you is stigmatized for many inmates. Many don't trust prison doctors – sometimes for good reason – so a large segment of the prison population will never have a clue as to whether or not they're infected. Furthermore, they don't want to know.

Therefore, some have estimated – or guesstimated, since there really is no way to know – that the prevalence of hepatitis C infection among the prison inmate population is somewhere between 39 and 54 percent.[36] By those guesstimates, literally every other person in prison could be infected. Who would want to play those odds when trying to find a healthy infection-free organ or tissue?

Then there is AIDS. Here is that scary statement again. "No other institution in this society has a higher concentration of people at substantial risk of HIV infection."[37] When this statement was made, over 20 years ago in 1992, the earlier mentioned studies conducted back then by the National Institute of Justice showed that the incidence rate of AIDS cases for the non-incarcerated general public was about 1 in 6700. However, state and federal correctional facilities reported one in 500.[38] Prisoners were infected with AIDS 13 times more per capita than the rest of the U.S. population.

As we learned, that number has dropped drastically since then. Twenty years later, it is now estimated that prisoners are infected with AIDS only about 1.7 times more than the rest of the U.S. population. That doesn't mean that the stats are that much less scary, though. Who would go into an area where you're more than twice as likely to catch any disease? Each year, an estimated 1 in 7 persons living with HIV will pass through a correctional facility.[39] Prison may actually be the number one destination for HIV carriers. True, most of the HIV carriers amongst the prison population acquired it outside of the prison setting. Nevertheless, incarcerated populations have far more risk factors that are associated with catching and transmitting HIV than most other communities in the U.S.

Moreover, much like hepatitis, many carriers of the HIV virus don't know they're packing such a deadly infection in their bodies. The CDC estimates that of the 1.1 million Americans carriers of HIV, 207,600, or 1 in 5, don't know they have it. How many of those unknowing ones are prisoners?

It was because of numbers like this that the Food and Drug Administration (FDA), since the early 90's, has advised blood and plasma clinics not to accept blood donations from prison inmates. It's due to that stated concern that the organ donation community has likewise been reluctant to accept organs donations from inmates. The risk of infection is very real. You won't find an argument against that here. While there are tests to ferret out those who are infected, the quote from DHHS at the outset of this chapter stands true. "No test is 100% accurate."

So, again, why would anyone want to risk getting an infection of AIDS or hepatitis from a prisoner?

Well the answer lies in what we discovered about areas around the country, outside of the prison setting, that are actually at a greater risk for disease transmission than from prisoners. The transplant community certainly doesn't shy away from accepting donations from the major metropolitan regions of the U.S. – hotbeds for infection compared to the rest of society. In fact, they instead oftentimes focus efforts to raise donation rates in these areas. How do they justify this and ensure that disease doesn't further spread from these regions?

Adequate testing is the answer. Tests may not result in a perfect 100% accuracy. But you may be surprised to know exactly how accurate they are, and how the transplant community ensures that donations are safe even from the riskiest environments.

If appropriate testing can be done in these areas, logic should have it that we can likewise adequately test each potential inmate donor to a satisfactory degree, right. Unfortunately, not in the eyes of the transplant community. But the only reason given for this continues to be that "no test is 100% accurate." It is, therefore, vital to gain an understanding of why that is before we get to some of the less tangible reasons for opposition to prisoner organ donation.

History of Disease Transmission from Donor to Recipient

A 1991 investigation by the Centers for Disease Control and Prevention (CDC) determined that an organ and tissue donor, who had been properly screened and tested negative for HIV at the time of donation, had somehow infected several recipients with HIV. Panic ensued. How could this happen? This wasn't the first occurrence of disease transmission from a supposedly healthy donor to recipient, not even of HIV. But most transmission of this sort of infection occurred prior to 1985, before the implementation of donor screening. Even though organ transplants had been happening for years (the first kidney transplant was in 1954. The first U.S. heart transplant was in 1968), the governing body of all things transplantation in the U.S. were not established until the mid-80's. (Organ Procurement and Transplantation Network (OPTN) (1984) and the United Network for Organ Sharing (UNOS) (1986).) Too, at that time, HIV/AIDS was relatively in its infancy. Not much was known yet of how to test for this particularly deadly virus. Yet, even after appropriate screening measures were established, the transmission of disease still occurred – this first of which was the 1991 case.

The occurrence naturally raised questions about the need for better testing and additional oversight of organ and tissue screening and transplantation. What resulted was a published report entitled, "Guidelines for Preventing HIV through Transplantation of Human Tissue and Organs,"[40] which addressed issues such as donor screening, testing, on recommendations on who should be excluded as donors. Years later, however, it became apparent that the traceability of disease transmissions was woefully inadequate. Therefore, in 2005, the Disease Transmission Advisory Committee (DTAC) was established to identify and review all potential donor-derived disease transmissions. Its first findings (data tracked between 2005 and 2007) revealed a total of 30 donor-to-recipient infectious disease transmissions.[41] Most were rare infections that are not routinely screened for. However, there were four HIV and four hepatitis C infections that were transmitted to organ recipients from one deceased donor who shouldn't have been allowed to donate.

The donor-derived disease transmissions only accounted for .96% of the more than 44,000 donations that took place within this period. Therefore, the risk for infectious disease transmission may seem as small as to be inconsequential. However, as the end of DTAC's report emphasizes, "This OPTN effort in DTAC is critical for minimizing the chances that disease transmission will negate the otherwise lifesaving potential of each transplanted organ." Any risk of infectious disease transmission is significant, as it could mean the difference between life and death for the recipient. One of the above infected died.

It was proven again as recently as 2009, when an unsuspecting kidney transplant recipient contracted HIV from a donor in an unnamed New York City hospital. The male donor acknowledged that he had engaged in unprotected sex with another man, but he was screened and cleared for HIV. Yet, he still transmitted the disease – becoming the first live donor to do so in over 20 years.

We'll discuss how this happened below. But with examples like that, it's understandable why the transplant community remains extremely squeamish when making determinations as to who can be considered for organ donation. Are they perhaps being too vigilant, though? How do some diseased donors slip through the cracks? Learning more about the modern screening and testing practices in place today will reveal those answers.

How a Screened & Tested Donor Transmits Disease

As the CDC discovered while investigating the 1991 transmissions of HIV to several unfortunate patients, AIDS and hepatitis virus' appear to be great at hide'n'seek during their first few months of life. What the CDC actually discovered was that despite the virus being present in the donor's body, the test to ensure that there was no virus didn't see it because of a "window period".

The tests back then didn't have the capability of finding the virus itself. Testing wasn't yet that advanced. But up until this point, they didn't necessarily need to be. The first thing the body does once it detects invaders is to send out antibodies to combat them. Standardized tests in the early 90's simply looked for the buildup of these HIV or hepatitis-specific antibodies. Once these antibody troops were found, it was evident that a virus was present. No antibody buildup, no virus. Only this wasn't quite the case.

It turned out that these troops can be a little slow to form up against HIV and Hepatitis viruses – sometimes weeks, sometimes months. It's not as though the virus is all that great at hiding so much as the seekers tend to take their time. And since the testing only looked for these antibodies, it was possible for the virus to be running around free, wreaking havoc in the body, completely undetected. The donor got tested and was found to be virus-free in a vacation-like "window period" between infection and detection. A false-negative of the worst variety. The perfect scenario for a young budding virus.

So in the case of our 1991 tragedy, despite the thorough screening of the day, the virus languished in relative freedom from attackers and remained undetected. The donor could have been tested weeks before, or right up to the day of the surgery, and the virus still would not have been found.

This necessarily raised alarms in the transplant community, prompting them to make new recommendations. They did so, out of necessity at the time, not only in respects to how the potential donor was screened, but also in regards to who should not even be considered as potential donors, due to the yet unsolved problem with the window period.

In 1994, the CDC introduced a new set of guidelines that included "Donor Exclusion Criteria." The following is an excerpt from the CDC's report concerning who they recommended should excluded from donation of organs or tissue at that time:

DONOR EXCLUSION CRITERIA

Guidelines for Preventing HIV through Transplantation of Human Tissue and Organs CDC May 20, 1994

Regardless of their HIV antibody results, persons who meet any of the following criteria listed below should be excluded from donation of organ or tissues unless the risk to the recipient of not performing the transplant is deemed to be greater than the risk of HIV transmission and disease (e.g. emergent, life-threatening illness requiring transplantation when no other organs/tissues are available and no other lifesaving therapies exist.) In such a case, informed consent regarding the possibility of HIV transmission should be obtained from the recipient.

Behavior/History Exclusionary Criteria:

1) Men who have had sex with another man in the preceding 5 years.

2) Persons who report nonmedical intravenous, intramuscular, or subcutaneous injection of drugs in the preceding 5 years.

3) Persons with hemophilia or related clotting disorders who have received human-derived clotting factor concentrates.

4) Men and women who have engaged in sex in exchange for money or drugs in the preceding 5 years.

5) Persons who have had sex in the preceding 12 months with any persons described in items 1-4 above or with a person known or suspected to have HIV infection.

6) Persons who have been exposed in the preceding 12 months to known or suspected HIV-infected blood through percutaneous

inoculation or through contact with an open wound, non-intact skin, or mucous membrane.

7) **Inmates of Correctional Systems.** (This exclusion is to address issues such as difficulties with informed consent and increased prevalence of HIV in this population.)

The exclusion of prisoners, as well as the other six recommendations for exclusion from the donor pool, made sense back then. It was risky enough to allow donations when they couldn't definitively rule out the possibility of dangerous infections. Why add the riskiest groups into the mix as well? It would have been a matter of time before other infections slipped through. No sense playing Russian roulette with someone's future health if you didn't have to.

But these exclusions were posted two decades ago. Certainly medical advances have come far enough to make these unnecessary by now. In corresponding with the transplant community regarding why prisoners are typically not accepted as potential donors today, the preceding report and its recommended exclusions were referenced. The kneejerk reaction by the transplant community remains that prisoners just present too high a risk for infectious disease. (They also cite the parenthetical note concerning difficulties with informed consent, which we'll discuss in later chapters.) To them, the risk simply is not worth any potential for the saving of lives, despite advances in testing.

Perhaps we should see what those advances have been to see if their remains any validity to their restriction.

Shrinking the Window Period

Medical technology in screening for HIV and other dangerous infectious diseases has advanced so much that you can now buy take-home tests over-the-counter at your local pharmacy next to the candy aisle. Users swab saliva from their mouth with a jumbo Qtip, and in 20 minutes the test claims to be able to detect "HIV-specific proteins." Unfortunately, this is just a fancier way of saying that the test detects the buildup of antibodies to the virus. In other words, the diagnostics field has invented a faster, more private, way of checking for the virus in exactly the same fashion as they did 20 years ago. If you had sex last night, or last week, or last month with Mr. AIDS, the AIDS poster boy himself, or even if you were directly injected with the virus, this convenient home test would tell you that you were as clean as a virginal nun. It doesn't solve the window period dilemma. Over the years, the window period related to the antibody tests have shrunk – from 24 weeks in 1990, to 6-8 weeks now. But a donor relying on such tests could still pass on an as–yet–to–be–found infectious disease that is hiding out and languishing in their unsuspecting body.

Fortunately, however, a transplant team would never rely on such results to have the final say as to whether a potential donor is healthy enough to donate. That's because tests have now been developed that look for the actual virus itself. The antibodies were simply too slow to cooperate. So back in 2001, the first screening test was introduced that was able to detect the actual genetic material of the virus. Thanks to the Nucleic Acid Amplification Test (NAAT), a virus could be detected within 12 days of its immigration into the new body host. RNA testing further brought that window period down to as little as 5 days. There was still a window period where enough genetic material had to be built-up by the infectious invader to be detectable. But it was a much smaller window than the up to six months that it could take the antibodies to buildup enough mass to be found. Due to the nature of the test, it was now actually more likely to have a false positive result than a false negative. Of course, you may have an early onset stroke, learning that you have

HIV when you don't. But fortunately, this only occurred in roughly 3% of those tested, and the testing has improved to greater accuracy since then.

More positively, especially with the improvement of the tests, and the continued shrinking of the window period, the chance that a donor will be able to pass on an unknown infection has been drastically reduced. This has been the case for both HIV and hepatitis screenings, as they are essentially the same test, only designed to seek out those specific viruses. Because of the known span of the reduced window period, now about 5 days, testing can be done the week before the transplant and again immediately prior to surgery to rule out any chances of an HIV or hepatitis disease transmission.

The following is a history of the advances in HIV and hepatitis testing:

HIV and Hepatitis Testing	DATE INTRODUCED	DETECTS	WINDOW PERIOD
ELISA I	1990	Antibody	16–24 weeks
RIBA I	1991	Antibody	
ELISA II	1992	Antibody	9–10 weeks
RIBA II	1993	Antibody	
ELISA III	1996	Antibody	6–8 weeks
RIBA III	1997	Antibody	
Western Blot	1998	Antibody	4–6 weeks
Nucleic Acid Amp Test (NAAT)	2001	RNA (virus)	12 days
RNA Polymerase (PCR)	2002	RNA (virus)	7–13 days
RNA Target Mediated Amp (TMA)	2003	RNA (virus)	5–11 days

"Not 100% Accurate"

If the testing has improved so much, how is it that an HIV-infected donor was able to go undetected in our 2009 scenario of the New York donor who managed to infect his organs recipient? Could it be because of the statement at the outset of this chapter, that "no test is 100% accurate"?

Further investigation revealed that the hospital simply did not do it's ordinarily diligent job when screening the donor. There was a reason why the hospital was left unnamed in news reports. According to the investigation by the CDC and New York City and state health officials, the New York hospital tested the male donor 79 days before the transplant. When he showed no evidence of infection, they failed to re-test him just prior to the transplant surgery. This was despite the donor telling the hospital that he had engaged in unprotected sex with another man.[42] The high-risk behavior alone should have signaled more thorough testing by the hospital. But it failed in the timing of its screening. Appropriate screening practices would have easily prevented this terrible transmission event.

Because of this case, the CDC posted a new set of recommendations, asking all transplant facilities to test living donors no more than seven days before their organs are removed and transplanted. The CDC has also recommended the use of the latest RNA tests, to ensure that the virus itself can be detected within the shortest period of time possible prior to transplant. While most transplant hospitals were already following this diagnostic protocol, these guidelines were just adopted as policy this year by UNOS to better guarantee that mistakes like the one above do not occur again.

Yes, it is a true statement to say that 'no test is 100% accurate'. Perfection is elusive in just about all areas of medical science. That's why even when you get a flu shot, you have to sign a waiver after reading a two-page information sheet on "What you need to know" before getting the shot, with a provided 1-800 number hotline in case you didn't get enough information on it. But in the case of HIV testing, studies have been done to see just how accurate such testing has become.

In 2005, the U.S. Preventative Services Task Force reviewed the evidence regarding the risks and benefits of then modern screening. The authors of the results concluded as follows:

"... A large study of HIV testing in 752 U.S. laboratories reported a sensitivity of 99.7% and a specificity of 98.5% for enzyme immunoassay, and studies in U.S. blood donors reported specificities of 99.8% and greater than 99.9%."

In other words, while no test is 100% accurate, when considering modern testing – where a negative test result will now be correct more than 9,997 times in 10,000 – the CDC recommends that a negative test result be considered conclusive evidence that an individual does not have HIV... even in a prisoner.

A rational look at the modern advances in screening technologies should determine that the probability of lives being saved far outweigh the now infinitesimally slight chances of previously concerning infections. However, as we learned earlier, prisons are a high-risk environment. And we saw what happened when the transplant industry has a lapse in protocol when considering high-risk donors. Should this preclude inmates from being able to be organ or tissue donors, perhaps out of an abundance of caution?

Safe Enough to Allow Prison Donors?

With the advancements in testing, have all concerns regarding disease transmission from donor to recipient been resolved sufficiently to now allow for even high-risk inmate donors? The simple answer is that as long as the appropriate testing has been done on the potential inmate donor, and the inmate donor has proven to be healthy, infection-free, and meets all other basic criteria for organ donors, and then the inmate can give his body parts for the lifesaving benefit of another as safely as any other prime donor candidate.

Fully aware that prisoners present a high risk for the spread of infectious disease, most prison systems today are extremely diligent when testing prisoners for HIV and hepatitis. Typically, there is a focus on prevention and screening efforts made by an expert HIV/ HEP coordinator to ensure that the most appropriate protocols are followed to prevent the spread of these viruses. When it comes to the potential for organ donation, it is reasonable to expect that such care will be at least as, if not more, diligently pursued.

The only residual concern would be to ensure that another 'unnamed New York City hospital' incident does not occur. Currently, for non-organ donation-related screenings, most facilities -- prison and medical alike -- still test for the AIDS and hepatitis viruses using the not-very-conclusive antibody test. Testing for the actual virus is typically only used as a confirmatory test after an antibody screening has produced a positive result. The reason for not first administering the more conclusive RNA test for the virus itself is due to cost factors. Antibody screening tests cost in the $5-10 range, whereas viral-RNA testing ranges from $50-295.

However, as explained by one Department of Corrections HIV/HEP Prevention Coordinator, when it comes to a potential inmate donor, they would follow the regulations as set out by the transplant policy-makers. As we learned earlier, the latest regulations call for testing for the actual virus prior to any donation. Regardless, with a transplant team involved, as would be a certainty with any organ donation, along with the heightened scrutiny afforded by the status as a high-risk donor, it is assured that every screening precaution would be carefully followed.

As the above Prevention Coordinator acknowledged, "If a person has both antibody and viral-RNA testing, and both are negative, there is no reason to believe that such person's organs, tissue, or blood products are infected with any communicable disease of interest."

Conclusion

Given the modern advancements in screening technologies, there is no reason that an inmate should be summarily precluded from organ donation over concerns of transmitting infectious diseases. Testing has now surpassed the concerns regarding the risk of prisoner organ donations expressed two decades ago, and appropriate oversight has now been established. Prisoners, regardless of the environment they live in, can now safely donate healthy organs and tissue.

However, the health of the prisoner donor isn't the only concern expressed by those opposed to inmate donations. The public health analyst from the U.S. Department of Health and Human Services quoted at the outset of this chapter had much more to say. Since most correctional institutions, courts, and transplant professionals will defer to this organization as the expert in the field of all things organ donation, it is necessary to continue considering each of the objections to prisoner organ donation carefully.

IS MODERN SCREENING GOOD ENOUGH TO APPROPRIATELY TEST WILLING INMATE DONORS FOR INFECTIOUS DISEASES?

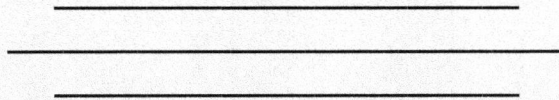

_____

_____

_____

FACTS:

2001

THE YEAR APPROPRIATE TESTING FOR HIV INFECTION WAS INTRODUCED IN THE U.S.

99.7

THE PERCENTAGE OF ACCURACY OF MODERN TESTING FOR HIV AND HEPATITIS C.

13

THE TOTAL NUMBER OF YEARS THAT THE BAN ON PRISONER ORGAN DONATION CONTINUES TO EXIST, EVEN AFTER APPROPRIATE TESTING FOR HIV INFECTION IN THE U.S.

Chapter 5

Can Prisoners Even Consent to Organ Donation?

"The OPTN/UNOS Ethics Committee has also deliberated on many issues related to organ donations from incarcerated individuals, including: ASSURING APPROPRIATE INFORMED CONSENT FOR BOTH DONORS AND RECIPIENTS..."

–Continuation of the response from the Public Health Analyst
U.S. Department of Health and Human Services (DHHS)

– – – – – – –

Donor Exclusion Criteria:

Persons who meet any of the criteria listed below should be excluded from donation of organs or tissues...

7. Inmates of correctional systems –– THIS EXCLUSION IS TO ADDRESS ISSUES SUCH AS DIFFICULTIES WITH INFORMED CONSENT.

–CDC Guidelines for Preventing Transmission of HIV through Transplantation of Human Tissue and Organs, May 20, 1994

Would you agree to have a pandemic flu virus squirted up your nose? We're not talking about the dead variety that we use as a vaccine to prevent catching the flu that you might get this fall. I mean the actual living, guaranteed-to-infect-you/you're-going-to-be-puking-your-guts-out, sort of virus. Of course you wouldn't. Not by choice. But some prisoners have. For a study in 1957, when the Asian flu pandemic was spreading, federal researchers sprayed the virus in the noses of 23 "voluntary" inmates at Patuxent prison in Jessup, Maryland, to compare their reactions to those of 32 virus-exposed inmates who had been given a new vaccine. And this wasn't an isolated case.

Prior to the mid-70's, prison facilities often conducted non-therapeutic studies involving various infectious diseases. The medical field has always had difficulty developing treatments and vaccines quickly enough due to their inability to use human test subjects as early as they would like. However, in inmate studies, prisoners offered doctors the ability to administer actual disease to an actual living, breathing "volunteer" and could then diagnose and treat it at a far earlier stage in actual people once the "volunteer" developed symptoms of the disease.[43] They could, thus, learn a valuable amount of information about early detection and treatment of a variety of diseases through imprisoned human guinea pigs. It was a dream scenario for researching doctors.

Between 1963 and 1973, for instance, the Pacific Northwest Research Foundation conducted a study on the effects of radiation on "voluntary" Oregon inmates.[44] Known as the Heller experiments, conducted by Dr. Carl Heller for the Atomic Energy Commission, researchers sought to determine the human body's responses to various experimental regimens. Among them, the effect of radiation on human testicular functions.

From Holmesburg Prison in Philadelphia, between 1961 and 1974, Dow Chemical, and Johnson & Johnson made extensive use of prisoners to test various experimental drugs. In one of the studies, the "voluntary" prisoners agreed to have a layer of skin peeled off their backs, which was then coated with a searing chemical to learn the body's reaction.[45]

Researchers in the mid-1940s studied the transmission of a deadly stomach bug by having "voluntary" prisoners swallow unfiltered stool suspension. The study was conducted at the New York State Vocational Institution, a reformatory prison in West Coxsackie. The point was to see how well the disease spread that way as compared to spraying germs and having test subjects breathe it. The researchers' conclusion, incidentally: Swallowing it was more effective than breathing it.

Government researchers in the 1950s tried to infect two dozen "volunteering" prison inmates with gonorrhea at a federal penitentiary in Atlanta. The bacteria were pumped directly into the urinary tract.[46]

The late 1940s and 50s saw huge growth in the U.S. pharmaceutical and health care industries, literally, in some cases, on the backs of inmates. By the 1960s, at least half the states allowed prisoners to be used as human guinea pigs; experiments funded by both government and corporations. By 1972, the pharmaceutical industry was doing more than 90 percent of their experimental testing on prisoners. Officials acknowledged they were doing so because prisoners were "cheaper than chimpanzees,"[47] and they volunteered!

Eventually, somebody started to consider that perhaps this wasn't the most ethical of practices. In 1977 the Commission for the Protection of Human Subjects of Biomedical and Behavioral Research was formed.[48] This commission was established by Congress to make recommendations on issues involving experimentation on prisoners. The not-so-shocking concern was that inmates were being misused as test subjects, despite the fact that the inmates had "consented" to be experimented on. The Commission came to the conclusion that this was a practice that needed to stop. As they stated, "Although prisoners who participate in research affirm that they do so freely, the conditions of social and economic deprivation in which they live compromise their freedom." Put another way, as one Georgetown University Professor who maintains that the prison environment is inherently coercive, stated, "When persons seen regularly to engage in activities which, were they stronger or in better circumstances, they would avoid, the principle of respect for persons dictates that they be protected."[49] In other words, prisoners are subject to coercion by virtue of the circumstances of their environment and they should be protected from doing things they might not do if they were not in this environment.

The government responded with reforms. The U.S. Bureau of Prisons effectively excluded all research done by drug companies and other outside agencies within federal prisons. Shortly thereafter, one-by-one each state prison system followed suit.

Can Appropriate Consent Ever be Given by a Prisoner?

Inmates are certainly a vulnerable class of persons whose voluntary consent cannot always be assumed. The claim is that a person in an imprisoned state cannot make certain rational decisions simply because of their physical deprivation. It represents the possibility of such psychological instability that the prisoners' ability to reason is practically impaired. Therefore, it's said, that true and voluntary consent cannot be obtained.

Those against the notion that an inmate can freely decide life-altering decisions list a variety of factors including feelings of guilt, depression, grief, fear, hopelessness, loneliness or even boredom will cause prisoners to make choices that they would not otherwise make if they were not locked up. Arguably it becomes too difficult to evaluate how a person might have acted under a different set of psychological circumstances and to figure out what "makes sense," as a rational matter, for the prisoner. Does that mean that prisoners can never consent to anything related to their health or to organ donation?

Well, as it turns out, the ability to obtain appropriate consent from prisoners can easily be found in the various policies set forth by both the prison system and the medical fields. The Department of Health & Human Services (HHS) and the Food & Drug Administration (FDA) have promulgated regulations specifically governing experimentation, which include safeguards to ensure adequate consent by prisoners.[50] In addition to these general provisions, the Department of Justice Bureau of Prisons have issued regulations that deal exclusively with studies involving prisoners and of persons employed in the prison system.[51] Moreover, the medical community has provided an explicitly detailed method by which to obtain prisoner consent for any medical treatment.[52] Corrections societies include guidelines created for obtaining such consent.[53]

If prisoners can give consent to medical treatment generally, or even choose to exercise a constitutionally protected right to die or refuse medical treatment, which they can,[54] then they must be presumed to be capable of consenting to less vital issues.

The Government and medical community on down have been able to figure out how to ensure that the prisoner is freely agreeing to undergo whatever procedure or inconvenience is necessary for the inmate at the time, without concerns over whether they are volunteering inappropriately. Since that has proven to be the case, apparently, the issue isn't in obtaining appropriate consent from a prisoner, what is the problem? Apart from the fact that the inmates "volunteered" for all of the above-mentioned ill-advised experimentations and tests, all of those inmates experienced another common thread that widely influenced this supposedly voluntary decision. Payment.

Consent becomes an abuse, otherwise known as coercion, when it is coupled with any sort of perceived advantage or inducement that the prisoner may receive upon giving his consent. Do you think that even a prisoner would stand up and say, "Yeah, I'll take the gonorrhea!" if there weren't some sort of payment for doing so? No, an inmate is not likely to consent to something like medical experimentation without some incentive.

However, even the smallest inducement that makes the life of the prisoner more comfortable or simply adds something to the grind of day-to-day prison life can be an overwhelming enticement that no longer makes the decision truly voluntary. Something as simple as a cell move to the sunny side of the building or the ability to buy coffee on canteen is enough of an inducement for some inmates to make extraordinarily unwise decisions.

Exploitation through Coercion

It is established the prison population is a uniquely vulnerable one that is prone to exploitation by nature of incarceration and deprivation of certain freedoms. The histories of medical exploitation of prisoners referenced above become glaring cases in point.

The presiding rationale for claiming exploitation focuses on the presumably fallible decision-making abilities of the prisoner. In the case of medical experimentation on inmates, prisoners were given inducements to participate that were oftentimes so great, relatively speaking, that their participation in the medical research program was virtually coerced. For example, for voluntarily participating in the Oregon Heller Experiments in the 1960's, inmates were paid $5 per month for agreeing to radiation exposure, $10 per biopsy, and $100 for undergoing a vasectomy. Many prisoners could not afford to turn it down. In other cases, prisoners were offered pardons for their participation. Specifically recognized as factors that might further motivate an inmate to consent to participate in a research project was relief from the every day monotony, providing a source of income, securing good food, a comfortable bed and medical attention, or favorable parole considerations. The poor prison conditions, idleness, and the high level of pay relative to other prison jobs indicated that the participation of prisoners in the program was not exactly voluntary. The medical community, therefore, was exploiting these prisoners, through inducements and incentives, to become research subjects for studies that nobody else would subject themselves to under ordinary circumstances.

Because of that, from the point of government intervention, ethicists decried anything that involved consent from a prisoner, prisons became understandably gun-shy about any sort of "research" projects, and the medical profession, when they could help it, gave prisons a wide berth – which is certainly emphasized by the transplant communities stance against prisoner organ and tissue donation. If the transplant policy-makers initial knee-jerk reaction to prisoners as donors is to shout out the high-risk nature of prisons, a close second hasty response is to point fingers at the "consent" issue.

It is unlikely that a prisoner would ever consent to something invasive if he were not gaining something from it. In the case of a medical procedure, he is likely gaining his health. He can consent to that, according to prison and medical standards. In that case, he is not offered any other inducement besides the betterment of his physical or psychological well-being. But how about when it comes to the physical improvement of somebody else, through an organ or tissue transplant from an inmate. Can a prisoner still give his consent?

Consent & Organ Donation

Willing organ donations by prisoners cannot be construed in the same light as medical experimentation or research. It is not the medical community or the corrections departments who are requesting involvement with organ donations from prisoners. The inmates themselves are requesting to be considered as donors. They are doing so for other reasons, including altruism, not for some personal gain in freedoms or comfort level.

To avoid the negative perceptions associated with inmate organ donations and the issues of consent or coercion it is necessary to assure that the inmate who is about to give an organ has done so absolutely voluntarily and without any financial incentives whatsoever. Other states have considered inmate organ donation programs that offer "good time" type incentives to increase inmate participation. Doing so, though, reignites the original dangers of coercion and cannot be considered. If inmates do not receive any inducements or anything that can be regarded as payment for their gift, it cannot be argued that they were coerced in any way.

Even without outside incentives to participate in organ donations some might argue from a spiritual point of view that there is an internal motivation that is so intense that it influences the actor's ability to reason effectively and creates conflict between competing values, beliefs and desires. When a mental compulsion is so overpowering that it is considered irresistible, it renders the resulting behavior un-free, right? Because of the prisoners state of punishment for something that they have done wrong, their own need for redemption may "coerce" them into donating for fear that without such redemption they will further be punished in a spiritual sense. There would be some debate as to whether this is a wrong view at all. It should be noted, however, that the deciding factor for determining consent is whether a person would make the same decision were he not in this circumstance. Such "coercions" affect the daily lives and decisions of many religious persons not incarcerated and should have no further relevance here than would be considered for others who wish to donate.

Obtaining Appropriate Consent

Consent from willing inmates to donate organs will necessarily require a sure process. Because organ donation involves performing surgery on someone who is not sick or requiring the procedure for their health, the medical community has always regarded the issue of consent from the donor with a heightened sense of carefulness. We'll take a more in-depth look at the Hippocratic Oath later. But the physicians' mantra in that oath is, "First, do no harm." Taking an organ from a healthy person who doesn't have to give up that organ is essentially causing undue "harm" to that patient and has thus technically violates the oath that all doctors take. Therefore, the idea of living organ donation has always been an ethically murky issue.

To come to terms with this issue, the medical community ensures that each donor is very well aware of what they're about to get themselves into. They require that each prospective donor is, first, physically and mentally capable of making the decision to donate through medical and psychological evaluations. They then go through a specific process to ensure that the donor is exhaustively informed of every aspect of the transplant and donation processes, including the evaluation process, the actual surgical procedure – including post-operative treatment – the availability of alternative treatments for the would-be recipient, the potential medical or psychological risks to the donor, the national and transplant center-specific stats on how well, or not so well, it's gone for donors and recipients prior to them, the possibility that they may not be insurable, and more. Only after they are fully informed are the donors allowed to consent to donate.

These consent rules are already in place. An example for such appropriate consent can be seen through the criteria set forth as conditions for participation in the Medicare and Medicaid programs. Some excerpts of their criteria are as follows:

CENTERS FOR MEDICARE & MEDICAID SERVICES

DEPARTMENT OF HEALTH & HUMAN SERVICES

(CFR, Title 42, Chapter IV, Subchapter G -- STANDARDS AND CERTIFICATION
PART 482 -- CONDITIONS OF PARTICIPATION FOR HOSPITALS)

TRANSPLANT CENTER PROCESS REQUIREMENTS

482.90 Condition of participation: Patient and living donor

The transplant center must use written patient selection criteria in determining a patient's suitability for placement on the waiting list or a patient's suitability for transplantation. If a center performs living donor transplants, the center also must use written donor selection criteria in determining the suitability of candidates for donation.

(b) Standard: Living donor selection. The living donor selection criteria must be consistent with the general principles of medical ethics. Transplant centers must:

(1) Ensure that a prospective living donor receives a medical and psychosocial evaluation prior to donation,

(2) Document in the living donor's medical records the living donor's suitability for donation, and

(3) Document that the living donor has given informed consent, as required under 482.102.

482.102 Condition of participation: Patient and living donor rights.

In addition to meeting the condition of participation "Patients rights" requirements at 482.13, the transplant center must protect and promote each transplant patient's and living donor's rights.

(b) Standard: Informed consent for living donors. Transplant centers must implement written living donor informed consent policies that inform the prospective living donor of all aspects of, and potential outcomes from, living donation. Transplant centers must ensure that the prospective living donor is fully informed about the following:

(1) The fact that communication between the donor and the transplant center will remain confidential, in accordance with the requirements at 45 CFR parts 160 and 164.

(2) The evaluation process;

(3) The surgical procedure, including post-operative treatment;

(4) The availability of alternative treatments for the transplant beneficiary;

(5) The potential medical or psychosocial risks to the donor;

(6) The national and transplant center-specific outcomes for beneficiaries, and the national and center-specific outcomes for living donors, as data are available;

(7) The possibility that future health problems related to the donation may not be covered by the donor's insurance and that the donor's ability to obtain health, disability, or life insurance may be affected;

(8) The donor's right to opt out of donation at any time during the donation process.

A few prison systems have already attempted to establish guidelines to govern prisoner inmate donations. The most appropriate and thorough prison organ and tissue donation policy – from the Texas Department of Criminal Justice (TDCJ) – can be found in the Appendix of this book. They section governing consent is a good example of how prisons can structure their guidelines.

TDCJ – Organ and Tissue Donation – Policy E-31.2
Policy IV.

The transplantation team will be responsible for informed consent in writing. All donations a free and voluntary. The offender will receive no award or compensation in any kind for his donation, including but not limited to preferred treatment by the TDCJ or improved opportunity for parole. An offender may refuse a donation at any time or consent to a donation as long as he/she is mentally competent, and this refusal or consent will not affect reward or penalty for having done so. All consents must include the potential organ of donation and

whether the donation is to occur while the offender is alive or
at death.

In addition to the already established donation consent guidelines, a few inmate-specific criteria might be suggested to address prison-sensitive issues. For instance, additional counseling may be required to discover the nature of an inmate's wish to donate. Because added pressures do exist in the prison environment, it's vital to ensure that the inmate is not being extorted in some way, either by another inmate or even prison staff. To further assure that this is not the case, it may be wise to enforce a waiting period from the time of the request to the date of final consent to donate. An example of this can be seen in assisted suicide acts, such as Oregon's Death with Dignity Act (DWD). When a patient says they're ready to die and asks for the lethal prescription allowing them to do so, the state not only requires that the patient is evaluated for medical and psychological reason. The patient is also required to wait for weeks from the date of their request before given the prescription in order to allow them an adequate amount of time to reconsider the, obviously life-altering, decision.[55]

Another aspect that might be stolen from the DWD act for use in ensuring inmates consent for donation is the explicit wording to ensure that the patients' right to rescind is protected. The right to rescind is an important one and must be granted unequivocally.

Right to Rescind Request (Death with Dignity Act – ORS 127.845 § 3.07):

"A patient may rescind his or her request at any time and in any manner without regard to his or her mental state. No prescription... may be written

> without the attending physician offering the qualified patient an opportunity to rescind the request."

Finally, due to concerns with vacillation, an inmate who does choose to take back his decision to donate should never again be allowed the option to be a donor simply for the reason that it adds question to the prisoners' willingness.

If the prisoner makes an unsolicited decision to donate and meets similarly stringent criteria as is already required by the medical community, with a couple of additional safeguards, his voluntary choice to be an organ donor is absolute and clear. Whether as a general population prisoner or as condemned inmate upon execution, the issue of a prisoner's consent can be easily satisfied with carefully set guidelines from already established practices.

Conclusion

Concerns over truly voluntary consent from prisoners are very real and should be given careful consideration. History certainly proves that prisoners decisions are heavily influenced when offered incentives to obtain their consent.

While it is rare that an inmate will choose to undergo invasive procedures without some sort of financial inducements, there are many who are willing to give up an organ to save a life. They do so for reasons separate from prison life, reasons which have nothing to do with relief from boredom, providing a source of income, securing good food, a comfortable bed and medical attention, or favorable parole considerations.

Organ donation creates an opportunity for prisoners to give back to the community whose social norms have been violated and it provides an opportunity to help a fellow citizen who desperately needs help. Cultivating such a generosity of spirit can do much to rehabilitate criminals conditioned by a life of hardship who think only of themselves. The more that is being done to prepare an inmate for a positive reentry into the community benefits all involved.

Should the donor happen to be a death row inmate who is to be executed, allowing good to come out of an otherwise hopeless situation only heightens the benefit to the institution and the community in general. It also gives the condemned inmate a way to die with a dignity and humaneness that is not in any other way possible.

When you consider voluntary organ donation from prisoners who choose to donate without incentives, past practices involving exploitive research and coercive experimentation have no bearing. The benefits to the community, along with the potential benefits to the prison and the inmate donor, far outweigh other considerations or further dwelling on abhorrent past practices that do not apply.

When presented with the need for organ donations and the possibility of such donations coming from truly willing prisoner donors with nothing to gain but a satisfaction from helping another human survive, it is only rational that the possibility be given careful honest attention, avoiding pre-conceived ideas that may no longer be relevant.

PART TWO

Organ Donations after Executions?

"ORGAN DONATION FROM DEAD PATIENTS WILL ALWAYS BE A SENSITIVE MORAL ENTERPRISE. WE MUST NOT RISK ETHICALLY SULLYING THIS PRACTICE BY HARVESTING ORGANS FROM EXECUTED PRISONERS."

–KENNETH PRAGER
PROFESSOR OF CLINICAL MEDICINE
COLUMBIA COLLEGE OF PHYSICIANS AND SURGEONS

"REGARDLESS OF YOUR POSITION ON CAPITAL PUNISHMENT, THESE EXECUTIONS DO OCCUR AND VIABLE ORGANS ARE WASTED...FACILITATING ORGAN DONATIONS FROM DEATH ROW PRISONERS CLEARLY SERVES THE PUBLIC GOOD."

–MARRICK KUKIN
PROFESSOR OF CLINICAL MEDICINE
COLUMBIA COLLEGE OF PHYSICIANS AND SURGEONS

We have thus far discussed prisoners in general and the conflicts they face from the transplant community and prisons. However, there is a segment of prison society – which includes me – that would like to be able to donate their entire body of organs after death. The catch is that "death" comes by execution, as we are on death row.

Studies in the mid-80s revealed that just over half of the condemned would donate organs after execution if given the choice. And this was at a time when the possibilities of organ transplantation were just beginning to be recognized. A recent study just conducted by Western Oregon University polling Oregon's death row population found that 91.3% would donate to a family member in need and that 78.6% would be interested in donating to a stranger. In all, if executed, roughly 80% would donate their organs. Whatever their reason, death row prisoners would overwhelmingly choose to donate if given the option.

Now, however, it is not just the prison or the transplant community that takes issue. It is the anti-death penalty community and activists that want to be heard. Additionally, there is already a horrendous example of death row "organ donations" in China that everyone is quick to point to as a primary reason why organ donations after executions cannot happen. Furthermore, there are logistical issues to consider that some say will prevent such organ donations from occurring.

It is necessary for us to take in depth look at each of the issues to determine whether these are substantial roadblocks or mere hurdles.

Interlude

Salem, Oregon. July 2

Shari made it to graduation by pure strength of will. It was a beautiful graduation full of smiles and tears; tears which nobody else could really have known that they were made up of so much more than just the successful graduation of her first child.

At 38 years old, she had one more child to go. She needed another year, but here she was again in her ultra-sterile second home. She hadn't been back to this hospital since her heart attack. She fought her body back into submission and kept driving towards her goal. Her ailing kidney had been able to be kept a bit more in check thanks to a new diet laid out by her specialists that paid more attention to regulating the intake of protein and salts. She had even been able to switch to a home version of dialysis machine. It had been a godsend. Now her 4 hours of time every other day, tied to her machine she still called Norton, (they were bound by blood, after all,) could be spent in the vicinity of her two meanings in life. No sound was sweeter than their voices, no matter what they were saying. As above-average, yet somehow still typical teenagers, they couldn't always sound like angels directly from heaven itself. But they were near her, and it was wonderful.

For the past month or so, however, the forearm fistula used for needle connections to the tubes that directed the blood flow between her and Norton had begun to show signs of obstructive tissue growth and clotting – a sign that her kidney condition was worsening. Despite the more tolerable regiment with the whole machine and being able to make it to the first of her goals, she noticed that she was feeling more and more depressed each week. Knowing this too was one of the flags her doctors had told her to be aware of, and because she really was trying to listen more when they said to stop trying to drive 200 mph over the sinkholes of her condition, she decided to see one of her specialists the day after graduation. The doctor sincerely applauded her for proactively setting the appointment and showing up, and then promptly hospitalized her.

Shari's fortitude had finally been exhausted. It was as though her system said, 'we got you this far. You're on your own now.' She had no other choice. She would need a kidney transplant. It wasn't as simple as saying 'Yes' though. Although she was in a favorable spot health wise to potentially be able to recover okay from a transplant, she had only been well enough to make it onto the waiting list for a kidney a couple of months ago – a list that is at least three years long. Her doctors told her that they would see what they could do, but she could tell that even they weren't that optimistic. She was left without any control of her fate, grateful to have made it this far, but with an internal fire still burning hot to go a little further. She felt like a freight train with enough fuel to go the distance, but that derailed and stuck in the mud. All she could do now was just lay there and pray for a miracle, knowing that she may not be able to make it through the month.

(Blood Type: B-positive.)

--

One floor down and a few identical rooms further down the hall was a 43-year-old loving wife and mother of three teenagers, and a successful account executive from Intel. Leah was similarly lying there, drowsily staring into the shadowy area that led off to the bathroom that was attached to her semi-private room. The pillows propping her up did little to ease the short quick gasps of her labored breathing.

Mild symptoms began about nine months earlier. Increasing weakness, shortness of breath, and anxiety over heart palpitations caused her to seek a medical opinion, even though she was sure that it was probably just stress. The doctors were baffled by the nonspecific findings from the physical examination. But ominous changes in the ECG tracing convinced them that it was some kind of heart disease.

Leah was hospitalized for definitive testing. An accurate diagnosis could only be approximated through a process of elimination. Two days of routine and highly sophisticated tests and procedures indicated the probability that she had a sick heart muscle, otherwise known as cardiomyopathy. That was a few days ago. Absolute bed rest was ordered and medications were introduced, but they did little good in controlling the increasingly frequent disturbances in her heart rhythm. Weakness and shortness of breath grew worse. Now all signs led to early heart failure. Doctors know that the course of this disease is unpredictable but usually short and grim. In her case it was extremely rapid, and the prognosis bad – in fact hopeless if she didn't get a heart transplant soon.

(Blood Type: A–neg.)

--

Eugene, Oregon. July 3

Fifty-three-year-old Harold was comfortably seated in his reclining chair at home, watching late-night TV with this wife and should-have-been-moved-out-by-now son, but also with the joy of his life four-year-old granddaughter on his lap. Despite the pleasant setting, his obvious distress is manifested by rapid and shallow breathing which, together with the oxygen tube in his nose, compels him to speak only short, Morse code-like phrases with a subdued voice. Even his grandbaby had learned that "pa-pa's" long stretches of silence were necessary and understandable. She could often be found in the comfort of his arms, as though she were there to help him if he needed it.

Many years ago, Harry, as everyone knows him as, sensed a gradual shortness of breath, sometimes with a mild dry cough. Occasional "colds" made the coughing worse, at times accompanied by wheezing. He began to lose weight a little too quickly too; but it was the shortness of breath that concerned him most.

A thorough medical exam six years earlier, including x-rays and lung function studies, revealed abnormally large clear spaces, some of them huge, in both lungs. Their functional capacity was severely diminished. The diagnosis was chronic obstructive pulmonary disease (COPD), better known as emphysema. In Harry's case, the cause wasn't really clear at first. He had only smoked cigarettes as a kid, to look cool at the bus stop (barely a pack a week for a semester.) But a lab test now revealed that he lacked an important enzyme known to protect against the onset of this particular disease.

Treatment had merely been supportive with oxygen, antibiotics and inhalers to help him control the ever worsening wheezing on prolonged exhalation of each troubling breath. Lately it had gotten much worse though.

Doctors concluded recently that his only hope was to have a lung transplant as soon as possible.

(Blood Type: A-neg.)

--

Albany, Oregon. July 5

A thin, well-developed nineteen-year-old man, Braxton, falls into a light sleep in a hospital bed adjusted to a near-sitting position. But bed rest and oxygen supplied by a nasal tube cannot alleviate hi labored breathing. Short gasps are accompanied by marked motion of a thin chest wall coarsely corrugated by a prominent ribcage. Due to the lack of oxygen in his blood, his skin looked more cadaverous than youthful. His anxious face underscores the constant hunger for air and the hopelessness he has begun to feel.

It all started three years ago with the usual mild and vague symptoms of weakness, fatigue, and loss of appetite. As a varsity basketball player, it was most obvious during games, some of which he had to warm the bench for because of feeling especially affected by whatever his ailment was. About a year later, he began to feel dull aches in his chest. Occasional coughs were usually dry, but sometimes produced yellowish projectiles. His doctor prescribed treatment for bronchitis, after which the coughing disappeared for several months. But when it showed up again, the mucus was streaked with a small amount of blood. That's when the doctor admitted him to the hospital for intensive investigation.

Besides being anemic, Braxton had significantly reduced functional capacity of his lungs. Fresh blood was detected in lung fluid. Microscopic evaluation of a thin needle biopsy through the thin chest wall confirmed a rare diagnosis: 'bleeding and deposits of blood pigment in the lung tissue beginning to undergo scarring, cause unknown.'

There was no specific or curative treatment. Oxygen helped his breathing, and antibiotics cleared up the bronchial infection, which allowed him to stay at home for long periods of time, without being able to do much in the was of the sports he loved however. But he had to be hospitalized again when he became very short of breath and a concerning amount of blood was coughed up a few days ago. Supportive therapy has been continued, but it's obvious that his disease has progressed to a very dangerous stage. Doctors are sure that he won't last long.

(Blood Type: A-neg.)

--

Portland, Oregon. July 5

Ridley languishes between semi coma and sleep in a private hospital room overlooking the Columbia River. Three years earlier, the married forty-one-year-old gaming engineer, husband, and father of a small son and infant daughter began having vague, nonspecific symptoms: headache, poor appetite, nausea and extreme muscle weakness. Shortly thereafter, a yellowish tint appeared in the whites of his eyes. A medical checkup later revealed a mild fever and more pronounced yellow-tan discoloration of the entire skin. In addition, there were bulging and irregularly tortuous veins on the abdomen; and his stool was pitch black.

On the second day after entering the hospital, Ridley vomited a small amount of dark red blood. X-rays showed the source to be dilated veins in the esophagus. His liver was small, hard, and slightly tender. A needle biopsy yielded the conclusive answer: 'Severe atrophic cirrhosis with extensive scarring.' Most of what was left of the functioning liver tissue showed signs of impending degeneration.

The exact cause of the devastating process was obscure. Ridley had never been a heavy or even moderate drinker. About twelve years earlier, though, he had a severe attack of the flu, which his doctor at the time thought was infectious mononucleosis.

His current prognosis is not good. It is obvious that without a liver, he won't last long. His name has been on the waiting list for a new liver for several months. Prospects seem dim to nil.

(Blood Type: A-neg.)

--

Death Row, Oregon. July 6, 11:28

"This is ridiculous!" the condemned man shouted at the man who had no power to fix it. "It's all the way wrong! Worse, man, it's cruel. And not to me. I don't matter. It's cruel to those people who won't even get the chance to survive. And for what? Because they don't want to set the precedent of using executed prisoners' organs for transplantation? Seriously? C'mon, it's not like they're killing me for 'em. I'm checkin' out regardless. My appeals are done. I asked to donate! Every part of me is healthy and can be used! Dammit!"

He had never been this angry during his 12 years on death row. Most of the issues he had to deal with in prison were either handled easily enough or they just couldn't be handled. He learned a long time ago not to get too worked up by anything that was beyond his control. He felt like his case was one of those things that fell into the latter category. He did what he did to get here, maybe not exactly how or why they said he did. But he did it. It took him awhile, but he finally came to terms with the reality that he would have to pay for it. Only, he never felt like he was "paying". The closer he got to his execution date, the more he felt like he owed more. Not a frequent thought from a death row setting; but not a totally uncommon one either.

"Is there anything you can do?" he pleaded with the chaplain. But he already knew the answer. The chaplain was sent at this stage of the game for comfort and calming, not for problem solving. It was far too late for that.

The chaplain was already shaking his head in similar disgust of the situation. The fact is that he had already tried to reason with the superintendent of the prison. But the warden had already made up his mind, and he had a slew of excuses to support his decision.

"I know, you're right," the chaplain agreed, trying to hide his own anger. "But there's nothing I can do. I'm sorry."

In his frustration with the prisons decision, he had almost forgotten about the letters that were sent with him to give to the inmate. He assumed that they were from family, maybe the woman he had been writing for all of his years here. But as he prepared to hand them to the condemned man, he could see that they were instead from the administration and one of the local hospitals. He suddenly wasn't so sure that he wanted to give them to him. But he was obligated.

"I was told to give you these," he said with obvious reluctance.

The inmate snatched them a little more angrily than he meant to. But when he saw that the top one had the far-too-familiar Department of Corrections letterhead, he felt justified in the involuntary display of anger.

"Dear Sir: After much deliberation and weighing the consequences of your requests to donate your organs and tissue for transplantation after your execution, I must inform you that I cannot accommodate your request. This is certainly a noble and humanitarian gesture by you. However, upon consideration of the legal, operational, social and policy implications, the interest of the public and condemned inmates are best served by denying your request. Respectfully..."

Swearing wasn't his way, especially in front of a chaplain, but he cursing up a storm in his head. The chaplain could see the contempt the rejected inmate was feeling by the way his jaw seemed to be flexing on its own and the way he kept stretching his neck. He understood his consternation more fully as he was handed the letter.

The second letter also looked official, although the condemned man didn't recognize it at first. Seeing though that it was from a medical center, be braced himself for more disappointment.

"Dear Sir: At the request of our chief of transplant surgery, I am responding to your recent letters to him. As no state has allowed donation of organs under your present circumstances, and there are no laws or precedent to guide your request, we regret to inform you that we cannot accept your donation. However, you are certainly to be commended for your wish to help in this regard. Sincerely..."

Already beginning to accept that this was going to turn out to be one of those things that he wasn't going to be able to do anything about, his seething and contempt started to subside back down to mere anger and irritation. He handed the letter to the chaplain to read as he started to flip through the rest of the photocopied letters brought to him. He had sent letters to everyone he could think of to try to get his organ donation wish accepted, so he figured he'd have a few more rejection letters in the pile. He was just wondering if the governor had maybe responded when he came across a letter from Shari.

"Hi Honey: I know it's been awhile and you're probably trying to take my absence in stride, joking that I'm your "hummingbird" –

impossible to catch. But you know how it is. Everything is crazy as always, never a moment to breathe, much less have a little time to myself to share with you. The truth is, though, you caught me a long time ago. I think about you all the time and I always mean to write to tell you about my day, but life intrudes. I'm sorry, but of everyone, I know you understand most of all.

Speaking of my days, I'm back home again. They've put me on hemodialysis, which is good and bad. But being able to bring Norton home has made it a lot easier to watch my babies grow up. They're so grown up; I wish they'd stop it already. But I have amazing news, which knowing you, you already figured out (or maybe the photo I put in here tipped you off,☺.) My firstborn is now officially a graduate of South Salem High School! She made it! I made it, babe! One down, one to go..."

He broke down before he could finish. He couldn't keep himself from it if he tried. Part of it was the rollercoaster of anxiety from the organ donation rejections. Part was because she wrote after months of invisibility, which he was kind of used to. But his wish to donate was motivated wholly by her and the possibility that he might be able to improve her life, maybe even save it, with a part of himself. He wanted nothing more than to help her in any way he could, but especially so that she could make it to her children's graduations and beyond. And now she had made it, to the first one. He was happy and sad at once, with an icing of pain that he couldn't see her now – not even the picture she had evidently sent was here!

Reading further, after marshalling his emotions, he began to seethe. She was back in the hospital, this time for her kidney. She wouldn't say it, she never did, but he knew that this time it was serious by how vague she was being. She never wanted to be too specific, since he would relentlessly pursue a fix, no matter how improbable. It was actually annoying to her just-press-on ways. Plus, she wanted to keep him from being tortured by something that he couldn't do anything about. A while back, just by comparing medical records, they discovered that they weren't a blood match. He was A-negative. She was B-positive. He couldn't donate his kidney to her if he was allowed to do so. Where he usually tried to not dwell on what he couldn't change, he was constantly trying to find ways that he could still affect the donations that would find her the organ she needed. When it came to her, he wouldn't stop trying. When they last spoke, he was talking about "paired exchanges" that would let him donate to somebody else who had someone in their life who wanted to donate but couldn't, due to blood-typing issues. They could find one that was a match for her and essentially swap – the 'swinging' of the transplant field. But she knew it wasn't likely to happen, so she avoided the topic when she could.

To him though, now, this rejection of his intent to donate became personal. The state was killing not only him, but they may also be killing her. He knew that the swapping option was doable. If there was better organization and people with the balls to help make it happen, it could happen. But no! Instead, they'd rather dodge the issue because it hadn't been done with a death row inmate! "There was no precedent." They were evading it because it was too controversial. What if it was their wife of daughter who needed the kidney? What if they knew that their loved one might not make it past the next year or the next month? What about the other seven or eight other lives that could be saved with just a say-so? They had just, by the stroke of a pen, and a distinct lack of courage, had just signed the death sentences of eight people! But I'll bet they won't lose a wink of sleep tonight over it.

"We're ready now!" His internal tirade was abruptly interrupted by two guards standing on either side of the chaplain at the cells opening door. He was so completely lost in the absurd tragedy of the situation that he had forgotten about his impending execution. His hands started to shake as he handed the chaplain the letters he hadn't had time to read. In the stack was a letter from somebody's brother who was looking for a match for his dying sibling. He was willing to do a "paired exchange" if it could be organized in time. He was B-positive.

--

Oregon Execution Chamber. July 6, 00:15 A.M.

What happened in the next hours is more than just plausible. Every time a prisoner is executed, one who was prevented from willingly donating their organs and tissue, this happens. The condemned man dies with a body full of organs and tissues that could have been used to save up to eight other lives and enhance the lives of up to fifty others with other usable parts... thus likewise condemning the ones that his body could have been used to save.

In this case:

A 43-year-old wife and mother of three daughters was condemned to death by heart failure.

A fifty-three-years-young grandfather was condemned to death by lung failure.

A promising nineteen-year-old was condemned to death by lung failure.

A forty-one-year-old husband and father of a small son and infant daughter was condemned to death by liver failure.

A brother of unknown age, who could have been saved by a paired exchange, was condemned to death by renal failure.

A thirty-eight-year-old mother, who lived solely for her teenage son and daughter, was condemned to death by renal failure.

All died unnecessarily. This invisible human tragedy happens almost every week in this country... needlessly.

IS CONSIDERING DEATH ROW DONORS EVEN WORTH IT?

_____

_____

_____

FACTS:

3108

THE TOTAL NUMBER OF DEATH ROW PRISONERS IN THE U.S.
(MID-2013)

1281

THE TOTAL NUMBER OF EXECUTIONS IN THE U.S. SINCE 1984

(THE FIRST YEAR THAT LETHAL INJECTIONS WERE USED.)

45

THE AVERAGE NUMBER OF EXECUTIONS ANNUALLY IN THE U.S.

52

THE PERCENTAGE OF U.S. DEATH ROW PRISONERS WHO WOULD LIKE TO
HAVE THE OPTION OF ORGAN DONATION AFTER EXECUTION.

2,644

THE NUMBER OF LIVES THAT COULD HAVE BEEN SAVED WITH ORGANS
FROM WILLING HEALTHY EXECUTED PRISONERS SINCE 1984.

(ASSUMING THAT ONLY HALF OF THE WILLING DONORS WERE HEALTHY ENOUGH TO DONATE. UP TO 8 LIVES SAVED PER HEALTHY DONOR)

CHAPTER 6

China's Bad Example

"TO ACCEPT ORGAN DONATION FROM AN EXECUTED PERSON "...WOULD BE REMINISCENT OF AN EGREGIOUS VIOLATION OF HUMAN RIGHTS AS WHEN THE CHINESE EXECUTED SCORES OF PRISONERS AND HARVESTED THEIR ORGANS TO FUEL A LUCRATIVE TRADE IN ORGAN TRANSPLANTS."

–KENNETH PRAGER

PROFESSOR OF CLINICAL MEDICINE
COLUMBIA COLLEGE OF PHYSICIANS & SURGEONS[56]

Almost universally, on the mere mention of using the organs of a death row prisoner, the knee-jerk reactionary statement has something to do with China's yanking them out of non-consenting death row inmates. Opponents of organ donation after executions cite this glaringly bad practice as a primary reason for why such donations should not be allowed. As one commentator put it, "If the United States were to implement such a system, the sale of organs would become a normal practice, the number of executions would rise without justification, and the organs of executed prisoners would be taken without consent."[57] Many state similar objections as they point to China and simply say "See!"

Therefore, it is important to review the history of China's example concerning organs from the condemned and determine if this presents a substantial roadblock in willing organ donations from those executed in the U.S.

China's Organ Crisis

China has one of the largest transplant programs in the world, peaking at over 13,000 transplants a year by 2004.[58] However, due in part to traditional Chinese beliefs, culture and a distrust of the medical system, voluntary organ donations are extremely rare.[59] For instance, Chinese customs call for people to be buried or cremated with their organs intact. It's obvious how this could pose problems for organ transplantation. Further, where in the United States we have organizations such as UNOS, the Red Cross, BeTheMatch and other organizations to rally support for organ donations, China has never really had such concerted movements.

For many years, China resisted even passing national legislation for organ donation or for establishing specific criteria to designate when organs could be ethically and medically taken, such as when brain death occurs. The worry was that in poorer areas of China, or areas with lax or particularly corrupt law enforcement, doctors would be tempted to act prematurely in declaring people to be brain-dead in order to harvest their organs.

China's cabinet, the State Council, finally issued regulations in 2007 for voluntary organ donations. But it has struggled to popularize the practice. In 2011, China's legislature adopted changes to the country's criminal code to specifically ban the forced removal of organs, showing that China is very much behind most modern countries when it comes to the organized regulation of organ transplantation. As with virtually every other country in the world, the need for organs far exceeds the supply. However, nowhere else in the world is this felt quite as severely as China.

For example, on average in the U.S., about 1 in 7½, or around 13%, of those waiting in line for organs will receive them. In China, where about 1½ million people are in need of a transplant annually, only about 10,000 will be fortunate enough to get them. In other words, only around 1 in 150 will get an organ in time to save their life. Less than 1% of those who need them will get an organ transplant in China. It's no wonder why China went looking for other, less palatable to Westerners, option for finding the organs needed to save its citizens lives.

History of China's Use of Organs from the Executed

The Chinese government has repeatedly denied that it has ever harvested organs from death row inmates without the explicit consent from the prisoners' families.[60] Despite such assertions, international human rights groups and activists began uncovering China's black market organ sales extensively in the early 1990's, spotlighting China's practices for western nations for the first time. Independent investigative reports repeatedly showed that such practices were indeed taking place. These reports prompted the official Chinese Press to publish the following statement: "Since in China there are relatively few donors of human organs, some medical units and People's Courts get together and use the opportunity of the execution of criminals to retrieve organs of executed prisoners without obtaining the agreement of prisoners' families."[61] However, Chinese government officials later refuted these statements.

In 1997, the FBI had cause to investigate allegations of organ harvesting in response to information obtained by the Justice Department.[62] The added scrutiny prompted news programs such as ABC's Primetime Live to further expose China's practices to the American public, which elicited a strong response from Chinese government officials.[63] The Chinese embassy in Washington, D.C. maintained "the so-called sale of criminals organs in China is a deliberate fabrication with ill intentions," again denying that such organ harvesting was taking place.

In 2001, a congressional subcommittee in Washington DC rigorously questioned Chinese government officials regarding China's commerce in organs from death row inmates.[64] An official from the Justice Ministry did bend a little by admitting that trafficking of death row organs occurred but was infrequent and it was carried out with the "presumed consent" of prisoners when it did happen – inmates could opt out. However, during news conferences, the Chinese government continued to state that there was no black market trade of organs from condemned prisoners, calling such reports "sensational lies" and "vicious slander" against China.[65]

But then, physicians who had taken part in retrieving organs from the condemned came forward to reveal the atrocities there, such as Dr. Wang Guoqi who worked at the Tianjin Paramilitary Police General Brigade Hospital. Dr. Guoqi testified before the congressional subcommittee that his hospital would frequently sell organs to wealthy patients oversees. His superiors would often order him to remove the requested organs from the bodies of death row inmates, which he would do. Though he acquiesced to the majority of the orders, Dr. Guoqi drew the line when it came to non-death row prisoners who were still alive. His firm refusal to comply when asked to remove kidneys from a living prisoner ultimately forced him to leave China and to seek political asylum in the U.S.[66] His testimony was clear and detailed, yet China still maintained that this was all a fabrication.

At one time, experts estimated that approximately 90 percent of all organs transplanted in China came from executed prisoners.[67] However, according to 2009 data from the human-rights advocacy organization Amnesty International, an estimated 65% of China's "donations" came from prisoners, still resulting in tens of thousands of harvested organs.[68] According to Chinese law then, organ procurement occurred only if the prisoner's body is not claimed, if the prisoner had consented to the organ removal, or if the prisoner's family had given consent.[69] However, as the statement in the Chinese press made clear, these organs were removed regardless of consent. Families were rarely even informed that the prisoner's organs were being removed or that they have been transplanted into someone else.

Finally, continued pressure from the western nations may have caused some in China to buckle. At a 2006 conference of surgeons in Guangzhou, China, the Deputy Health Minister reluctantly acknowledged the flourishing sale of organs to foreigners and conceded that the source of these organs was, in fact, executed Chinese prisoners.[70] While the Deputy raised this information in the context of a call to stop the illegal trade, it was the first admission by a high-ranking official in China.

Soon thereafter, on March 28, 2006, China's Health Ministry officially banned the sale of human organs and strengthened regulation over organ transplants by mandating that organ donors give written consent, effective July 1, 2006.[71] Some speculated that the abrupt change in China's law might have been due to the scheduling of the 2008 Olympics to take place in Beijing, China. Already several human rights organizations had planned protests of various contentions with Chinese policies. In fact, prior to the Olympic committees acceptance of Beijing's bid to host the 2008 Olympics, a California Representative directed a resolution to the committee asking them to reject the bid based on China's record of human rights violations, notably citing the commoditization of death row organs.[72]

Pressure from the West finally seemed to cause China to change its policies on the nonconsensual removal of organs from death row inmates. In 2012, Huang Jiefu, the vice minister of health, announced plans to cease all reliance on organs from death row inmates within the next five years and China formally published legislation to show the world that it had taken supposedly proactive measures toward reformation.[73] Finally conceding officially that China had depended for years on executed prisoners as their main source of organ supply – as we already knew – the Xinhua News Agency quoted Mr. Huang as saying, "The pledge to abolish organ donations from condemned prisoners represents the resolve of the government."

It remains to be seen whether China has acted or will continue to act in accordance with its recent legislation. As Nicholas Bequilin, a senior researcher in Hong Kong for Human Rights Watch, pointed out, Mr. Huang, who turned 66 the year of the announcement, was about to retire, along with most of the country's top political leadership. That means that the next generation of political leaders and Health Ministry officials would have to deal with the problem of how to obtain enough organ donations voluntarily to offset the country's dependence on prisoners. It's also noteworthy that it was Mr. Huang that announced the ban in 2006, which apparently did nothing to actually eliminate the use of prisoners for their organs. As Sarah Schafer, a Hong Kong-based China researcher for Amnesty International, said, "Officials repeatedly make announcements every few years, but they don't appear to have a solid plan in place."

Thus far, there has not been an in-depth analysis or commentary on the results of this new policy. However, human-rights advocates doubt that China will be able to completely phase out the use of prisoners organs entirely. China is just too dependent on them.

Capital Punishment: China Compared to the U.S.

Those who favored the practice of organ harvesting from nonconsensual death row inmates argued that due to the prisoners' atrocious crimes, the personal rights of these prisoners could simply be revoked and the country could do as it saw fit with an inmate's organs after execution.[74] However, in China, "atrocious" crimes are relative. China doesn't publicly report its execution figures. But in a March 2006 report, Amnesty International stated that China executed 15,000 prisoners each year.[75] A more conservative estimate was made by the Dui Hua Foundation, a human-rights group in San Francisco, estimating the number to be closer to 8,000 executed in 2007, and reduced much further by 2011 to around 4,000 executed due to recent law changes authorizing the Supreme People's Court to conduct final review of death sentences handed down by lower courts. However, you cut it, the number of those sentenced to death and those who are executed is extreme – at least 100 times more than those that occur in the U.S. China authorizes the death penalty for sixty-eight separate offenses, including tax evasion and auto theft.[76] Amnesty International estimated that sixty-nine percent of the country's executable offenses were for non-violent crimes such as drug dealing and the open practice of illegal religions. Furthermore, the accused are often convicted after rushed trials based on confessions exacted under torture.[77]

China's executions are carried out without public notice or witnesses, oftentimes within a month of being sentenced to death. The prisoner is secretly executed by firing squad with a bullet to the head to maintain organ viability, the family is denied access to the body and the body is quickly cremated without autopsy.[78] Otherwise, little else is known about the process.

Reports indicated that healthy prisoners with useful organs were often bumped to the front of the execution waiting list.[79] Other reports stated that most of the purchased kidneys came from prisoners executed for minor offenses.[80] Some reports stated that executions frequently took place according to the current transplant needs, with monetary gain being a motivating factor in carrying out the executions.[81]

The organs from executed prisoners were often sold to the highest bidder, with some bids reaching $30,000. Dr. Guoqi testified that his hospital often sold organs and skin to wealthy patients – kidneys selling for up to $15,000 each.[82] Moreover, as discussed previously, all of this was done without the consent or even the knowledge of the prisoner, their family or in abidance with any strict organ procurement laws.

China's use of capital punishment differs dramatically from its use in the United States. Comparatively, the death penalty in the U.S. is reserved for only the most heinous and violent of crimes. It is only imposed after lengthy trials considering the mitigating factors of the crime and the history of the criminal. On average, only fifty-five executions occur in the U.S. per year, and only after a long series of appeals. Where a death row inmate in China might have a month to live after his sentence, the average length of the appellate process for a death row prisoner in the U.S. is 12.7 years – 10 years in Texas and 15–20 years in most other states.

The execution processes in the States differ in just about every ethical way from those in China. To say that we cannot do something because China set a bad example would have the U.S. abolishing the death penalty for fear of similar abuses. The two governments' capital punishment policies are not comparable.

Organ Donation: China Compared to the U.S.

As with capital punishment comparisons between China and the U.S., the two governments' policies on organ procurement cannot be compared. Unlike China's practices, organ donations in the U.S. are strictly regulated by the Uniform Anatomical Gift Act and its governing organizations.[83] While organ donation is encouraged, there is much oversight to guarantee that organ donation is solely by voluntary consent, that specific ethical policies are followed and that both the donor and recipients' rights are maintained in the process. The U.S. embraces an altruistic approach toward organ procurement law and, therefore, the sale of human organs is expressly outlawed.[84]

Also, while the need for organs is dire in the U.S., we in this country cannot begin to feel the desperation of those in need of organs in China. If the chances of getting a needed organ in China are less than 1% now, imagine what it will be without the ability to use prisoners for their organs. The odds of surviving death row are greater than that. Those who discover they need an organ transplant to survive are essentially getting an assured death sentence, with no rights of appeal or clemency. The situation here, while critical, is not so hopeless as to force anyone to donate, much less condemned inmates or other prisoners.

Part of the reason that organ donations from the executed are not occurring in the U.S. now is due to the caution exercised by the transplant community to adopt policies that protect the rights and safety of all U.S. citizens, even those who are sentenced to die. Simply the hint of impropriety by another country causes ethicists to discourage policies that appear to be leaning in that morally questionable direction, as with China's practices. In fact, some in the transplant community have classified a potential organ donation policy for the condemned as "morally repugnant".[85] While that classification is even debated within the transplant community, it proves the point that the approach of the United States towards organ donation policies is far more carefully considered and ethical than those of China, perhaps to a fault.

A Reasonable Consideration of Organ Donations from the Condemned

The unfortunate reality of such an atrocious organ procurement plan as China's should not undermine every organ donation program centered on prisoners who want to donate their organs. The transparency and the procedures of the legal and transplant systems in place in the U.S. already prevent the atrocities of China's system from occurring here. Simply by virtue of China's practices and the U.S. response to these practices demonstrates that this government will not tolerate such abuses within its borders. In that, China has become a poignant reminder of what not to do.

Any organ procurement policy regarding the condemned will necessarily center on the absolute willful consent of the condemned with several safeguards in place to ensure that this is unquestionably voluntary. Moreover, unlike China, organs shall not go to the highest bidder. Organs procured from the executed prisoner will only be available to those recipients who are registered on the national waiting list and in the set order that their name comes up.

The organ donation crisis is such that this country cannot afford to overlook any viable alternative, so long as that alternative does not conflict with the U.S. standards of human rights and decency. To forego the opportunity of taking the organs of a healthy but dying man who is offering them willingly and freely is a terrible waste of human life that could otherwise be saved. To decline this one gift of healthy organs is to unnecessarily guarantee the death sentences of six to a dozen others who do not deserve to die.

To follow the logic that the U.S. cannot consider organ procurement from the condemned because China -- a country known for vast human rights violations -- has set a bad example, is not sufficient rationale for disallowing consideration of organ donations from willing condemned inmates when such a program can be instituted in an ethical, safe and practical manner.

There are, however, some legitimate logistical considerations that seem to stand in the way of organ donations from the condemned. Without satisfying these, it is simply not possible for an executed prisoner to donate and therefore cancels the entire argument.

For instance, the execution process itself...

DOESN'T LETHAL INJECTION MAKE DONATION IMPOSSIBLE?

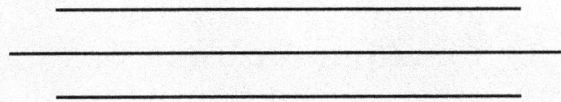

_____

_____

_____

FACTS:

3

THE NUMBER OF DRUGS USED IN THE OUTDATED LETHAL INJECTION PROTOCOL IN THE U.S., WHICH MAKES ORGAN DONATION IMPOSSIBLE.

1

THE NUMBER OF DRUGS NECESSARY FOR THE MOST HUMANE EXECUTION POSSIBLE UNDER ANY LETHAL INJECTION PROTOCOL.

(ONE-DRUG PROTOCOL ALLOWS FOR ORGAN DONATIONS)

13

THE NUMBER OF STATES CURRENTLY USING THE ONE-DRUG LETHAL INJECTION PROTOCOL THAT ALLOWS FOR ORGAN DONATION.

(OUT OF THE 35 STATES THAT STILL HAVE CAPITAL PUNISHMENT)

18

THE NUMBER OF STATES THAT HAVE OR ARE CONSIDERING THE SWITCH FROM THE THREE-DRUG PROTOCOL TO THE MORE HUMANE ONE-DRUG ALTERNATIVE THAT ALLOWS FOR ORGAN DONATION.

CHAPTER 7

Doesn't Lethal Injection Kill the Organs?

"THE PUNISHMENT OF DEATH SHALL BE INFLICTED BY THE INTRAVENOUS ADMINISTRATION OF A LETHAL QUANTITY OF AN ULTRASHORT–ACTING BARBITURATE IN COMBINATION WITH A CHEMICAL PARALYTIC AGENT AND POTASSIUM CHLORIDE OR OTHER EQUALLY EFFECTIVE SUBSTANCES SUFFICIENT TO CAUSE DEATH."

–TYPICAL STATE'S LETHAL INJECTION PROTOCOL...UNTIL RECENTLY.

When first deciding that I wanted to donate my organs after my execution, the first question wasn't whether it would be allowed. I naively assumed that the state would obviously want to put my healthy organs to good use if I volunteered them freely. I thought my biggest hurdle to accomplishing my goal was going to be the process by which they ended my life. I knew about the three-drug protocol, of course. Every death row inmate does, as well as we know our own state identification numbers. I figured, as do most when they hear that someone wants to their body to medicine after a lethal injection, that the poisons we are injected with would completely ruin my organs. I would somehow have to get the lethal injection protocol changed to allow me to donate healthy parts. At the time, I considered this my greatest challenge to my wish to donate.

I was right. Everyone is right. Organ donations are not possible under the typical three-drug lethal injection protocol. The combination of all three chemicals will cause the cessation of all cardiopulmonary function. The heart will stop pumping blood to the organs. The organs will be rendered useless immediately thereafter.

However, the "typical" three-drug protocol is not quite so typical these days. Due to several complications with what has been the norm in lethal injection protocols, it has been a necessity for executioners to come up with alternative protocols. Now, in all states that have actually executed inmates recently, the three-drug protocol that made organ donation impossible has now been replaced by a viable alternative which is not only makes it medically possible for organ donation, but that also allows the inmate to die in a more humane manner.

History of Lethal Injections

The concept of lethal injection as a method to put someone to death for the most egregious of crimes was actually first proposed over a century ago, in the early 1900s. It was proffered by a New York doctor who figured that it would be cheaper and far more humane to kill somebody by this method, as opposed to the then current practice of hanging.[86] Nevertheless, nobody took him up on his idea. Later, it was considered by the British Royal Commission on Capital Punishment (1949-1953), back when they believed in such a punishment, but it was eventually rejected after pressure from the British Medical Association (BMA.)[87] Shortly thereafter, the British decided against capital punishment altogether and haven't looked back. Not used for "capital punishment" per se, but noteworthy just the same, the Nazi government used a lethal injection process as one of its several methods of destroying what they dubbed "life unworthy of life." We know the terrible history surrounding that idea.

In the mid-1970's, after the reinstatement of capital punishment in the U.S., the state of Oklahoma was looking for a more humane method of execution than the macabre electric chair popularly used by most states up to that time. By 1977, Oklahoma's state medical examiner, Jay Chapman, thought he had the answer. He proposed a method by which a person could die as humanely as if they were falling asleep. What came to be known as the Chapman Protocol, Jay Chapman described his process this way: "An intravenous saline drip shall be started in the prisoners arm, into which shall be introduced a lethal injection consisting of an ultra-short-acting barbiturate in combination with a chemical paralytic." Sound familiar? After being approved by an anesthesiologist, Reverend Bill Wiseman introduced the method into Oklahoma legislature, where it passed and was quickly adopted. Since then, all of the 35 states using capital punishment have introduced almost verbatim lethal injection statutes. On December 7, 1982, Texas not so shockingly became the first state to test-drive lethal injection, and remained the most prolific user of the of what we know as the three-drug protocol, until recently.

To get a glimpse of the company we've kept in relation to this protocol, The People's Republic of China began using this same method in 1997, followed by Guatemala in 1998, the Philippines in 1999, Thailand in 2003, and Taiwan in 2005.

Why the Switch?

The three-drug lethal injection protocol has been around – and, according to death penalty proponents, used successfully – for over 30 years. Why the sudden about-face?

There are several reasons, actually, but it all began with a legal challenge by those against the death penalty who felt that the combination of the three drugs amounted to cruel and inhumane punishment of the condemned. The landmark case against the three-drug protocol is Baze v. Rees.[88] There the petitioner contended that the current method of execution presented a significant risk of unnecessary infliction of pain to the defendant. The basis for the arguments were various studies that had been done which seemed to prove that after the administration of the second drug of the protocol, the paralytic pancuronium bromide, the first drug was diluted. Thus, a proper amount of barbiturate may not be in the system by the time that the third drug, potassium chloride, is introduced to stop the heart. They pointed to euthanasia protocols and veterinary guidelines that prohibit the use of the same second drug due to its inherent dangers to the patient.

In total, petitioners argued that the effect of dilution or improper administration of the drugs is that the inmate dies an agonizing death through suffocation due to the paralytic effects of pancuronium bromide and the intense burning sensation caused by the last drug. However, through the injection of a single large dose of a barbiturate, the execution can be painlessly accomplished. They stated that any use of additional chemicals is superfluous and presents an unnecessary risk of pain.

The U.S. Supreme Court ultimately rejected the argument stating, "Given what our cases have said about the nature of the risk and harm that is actionable under the Eighth Amendment, a condemned prisoner cannot successfully challenge a state's method of execution merely by showing a slightly or marginally safer alternative." However, the Court stated at the conclusion of its opinion, "...our approval of a particular method (of execution) in the past has not precluded legislatures from taking the steps they deem appropriate, in light of new developments, to ensure humane capital punishment. There is no reason to suppose that today's decision will be any different."

Subsequent changes by Ohio and Washington to the single-drug protocol became cases in point. With the adjustment, those states were avoiding further litigation on the issue, but they were also adopting an evolving standard that would prove to be more humane in more ways than were instantly obvious to them. Most capital punishment states, however, declared the Baze standard as their excuse to keep the three-drug protocol in place. Even though the humane benefits of the one-drug execution were obvious to the Court, the Court said they weren't required to change it, so they didn't. That is until they were forced to make the change.

While the first drug of the three-drug cocktail simply called generically for "an ultra short-acting barbiturate," virtually every state used the same one – sodium thiopental. When the company who supplied the drug – Hospira – had temporary difficulty with the manufacture of a key ingredient to continue producing enough of the drug, a widespread supply shortage developed. In an effort to keep up with demand, Hospira planned to switch to an Italian manufacturing plant. Italian authorities, however, wanted a guarantee that the drug would not be used in executions, as Italy and all European countries are opposed to capital punishment. Fearful of the consequences if they agreed, but the drug somehow found its way to the gurney, Hospira stated, "We cannot take the risk that we will be held liable by the Italian authorities if the product is diverted for capital punishment. Exposing our employees or facilities to liability is not a risk we are prepared to take." With that, sodium thiopental no longer existed. (Coincidentally, at the beginning of the shortage of sodium thiopental, the U.S. Court of Appeals was reviewing a lower court ruling against the FDA concerning the illegal importation of the drug. As it turned out, the drug was never FDA approved. So by allowing the unapproved drug to be imported to the U.S., they were violating federal law. The Court of Appeals upheld the ruling.)

The decision left states scrambling for an alternative. Oklahoma became the first to find one – pentobarbital, the drug used to euthanize animals. It had already been approved as a sedative for humans, and was primarily used in humans for the treatment of epileptic seizures. Oklahoma simply just plugged the drug into the space left by the sodium thiopental, and carried on as normal. After all, Oklahoma developed the three-drug protocol in the first place. No sense abandoning it now.

Other states, however, due to the fact that they had to change their statutes and state administrative rules to accommodate for the use of a different drug anyway, decided to go ahead and make the switch to the more humane one-drug option. It turns out that most states didn't want to change to the one-drug option before this because it was just too much paperwork - well, and that it was largely untested before then. However, Ohio and Washington became the proving grounds for that. So now, as each state, that hasn't already made the switch, approaches its first execution since the old drug vanished, they rewrite their laws and regulations to accommodate the new drug and the more humane one-drug protocol.

After Ohio and Washington, Texas - yes, Texas - adopted the change, which likely has made it an easy decision for every other state to do the same. As of this writing, thirteen states have officially made the switch, including the aforementioned, plus Arizona, Arkansas, Georgia, Idaho, Louisiana, Missouri, North Carolina, South Dakota, Tennessee, and Kentucky (which is where Baze v. Rees originated. So even the state that won the right to not have to switch to the one-drug protocol switched.) The remaining twenty states, less stubborn Oklahoma, who have not made the switch simply have not yet had an execution yet to worry about going through the paperwork hassle. Who knows, maybe the "typical" protocol will change yet again in the meantime. No sense worrying about it now, is what I imagine their philosophy to be.

That reasoning may actually prove to be sound, as there are already supply problems again. It turns out that the primary supplier of pentobarbital, Lundbeck, a Danish company, isn't too keen on its drug being used as the primary execution drug. In a statement, Lundbeck said, "[We] do not condone use of pentobarbital or any other product for capital punishment." The company's president sent letters to the directors of Ohio, Oklahoma, and Texas prison systems urging the states to stop using pentobarbital in their executions. Spokespersons said the company was investigating what it could do to stop distribution to prisons for use in executions, short of pulling the drug from the U.S. market, which of course the opponents of capital punishment have been in full support of.

Texas' supply of pentobarbital ran out at the end of 2013, and as of this writing, they were having difficulty obtaining more supply. Missouri encountered a similar problem procuring the drug and instead made the decision to use propofol instead – the drug that made headlines as the sedative that killed Michael Jackson. Being yet another untested drug, however, Missouri has been fighting legal challenges to its use, which have already halted one execution in that state.

Some death penalty states, most recently Georgia, have announced they're turning to compounding pharmacies, which make customized drugs that are not scrutinized by the FDA, to obtain a lethal drug for execution use. These will undoubtedly face significant challenges before they are ever actually used for an execution.

Organ Donation & the Single Drug Protocol

With what most, including me, deemed to be the greatest obstacle to organ donation from executed inmates overcome now moved out of the way, is donation now simple, medically speaking? Not necessarily.

The single drug is a sedative that is administered intravenously to induce surgical anesthesia. The agent is quickly concentrated in the brain and rapidly causes unconsciousness, with a significant decrease in blood pressure and respiratory depression. Because of the decrease in blood pressure and depressed respiration, brain damage is likely to occur as soon as three minutes after commencement of the injection. The dosage, exceeding that which would normally be administered, would be sufficient to render the condemned brain-dead.

Because the inmate would die from the cessation of brain function, which is the legal definition of death, the organs would still be intact. It is possible that the heart can continue to pump blood to the various organs until which time they can be removed for transplantation. The procedure for this would be identical to that used regularly by physicians who procure organs from their brain-dead patients.[89] The inmate would be declared brain dead, thus officially deceased, and could then be ventilated and monitored to ensure the viability of the organs for healthy transplantation. Ideally, however, on-the-premises surgical facilities -- such as a surgical vehicle that many hospitals utilize for emergencies -- will be available for immediate organ procurement upon the declaration of death. One state lawmaker has recently tried to establish a similar procedure in his state, surprisingly for the state of Oklahoma. Representative Joe Dorman drafted a bill that calls for the inmate to undergo strictly controlled surgical depth general anesthesia – as used routinely in hospitals every day and therefore safe for organ procurement – induced precisely at the moment stipulated by law or by the court, have their organs removed right there at the prison facilities, and be kept on some form of life support until they can be officially executed. With this plan, however, doctors would not be waiting for the "patient" to be declared brain dead before harvesting the organs, thus potentially causing the medical community to balk at the plan.

Even if the inmate is properly, medically, declared brain dead, the death chamber removal of organs still does not come without hurdles. Given the complexities of anesthesia and organ procurement, physician participation would necessarily play a prominent role. The medical community may object to any physician involvement in the process of organ procurement as it has with participation in executions.[90] In addition, there will likely be the continued loud objections from the anti-death penalty community for reasons ranging from the issues in China regarding executions and organ procurement to the overall process seeming too humane and, thus, likely to prompt more juries to choose the death penalty over life in prison.

However, the procurement of organs from a death row inmate after execution, while logistically challenging, is entirely feasible. Since the infancy of organ transplants, physicians have figured out ways to procure organs from willing donors, even if they were on the battlefield in the middle of a war. It is not logistically impossible. It's just a matter of those with the knowledge and ability coming together to formulate a plan.

The original lethal injection protocol was created and first implemented in Oklahoma. Ironically, they may be the last one to use it. As more executions are occurring in the one-drug states without complications, other states have seen the obvious benefits of adopting the one-drug protocol and are likewise making it their primary method of execution in their states. Now, as far as lethal injection is concerned, the only real hurdle would seem to be in getting prison administration to allow for organ donations from the executed. There are still some logistical considerations and some ethical clouds, but what was once the greatest hurdle to organ donation from condemned inmates has now been removed. You will see in the following chapters that the remaining looming concerns are not really that concerning after all.

The following is a review of those battles, beginning with the states that have already adopted the one-drug protocol. As long as the death penalty exists, litigation over the method of execution will be there. The one-drug protocol is, by far, the most humane option to date, which still doesn't prevent it from being challenged. However, the tide of change to this protocol becomes obvious.

CURRENT LETHAL INJECTION METHODS IN THE U.S.

States with the newer one-drug lethal injection protocol	States that have already used the one-drug lethal injection protocol	States that still have the old 3-drug method on the law books	States that have continued to use the old 3-drug within the last year
Arizona	Arizona	Alabama	Oklahoma
Arkansas	Georgia	California	
Georgia	Idaho	New Hampshire	
Idaho	Ohio	New York	
Kentucky	South Dakota	Pennsylvania	
Louisiana	Texas	Indiana	
Missouri	Washington	Kansas	
North Carolina		Nebraska	
Ohio		Delaware	
South Dakota		Florida	
Tennessee		Mississippi	
Texas		South Carolina	
Washington		Colorado	
		Montana	
		Nevada	
		Oregon	
		Utah	
		Wyoming	

State's One-Drug Protocol History:
Those states that have used it

Ohio:

On Thursday, November 12, 2009, the State of Ohio became the first state to adopt a procedure for lethal injections that uses a single drug.[91] The adoption was made after several difficulties with and subsequent challenges to the conventional three-drug protocol.

Inmates executed using the one-drug method in this state: **13**

Washington:

On March 5 2010, the state of Washington became the second state to adopt the one-drug protocol. "The decision to amend the protocol was made in light of the three executions which have been completed in Ohio using a single dose of sodium thiopental, and in light of the opinions of the experts who have advised the department."[92] (Stephen Sinclair, Supt. WSP)

Inmates executed using the one-drug method in this state: **1** (9/10/2010)

South Dakota:

On October 21, 2011, the state of South Dakota became the third state to adopt the one-drug protocol. The revised protocol permits the Warden to choose between a one, two, or three-drug protocol.

Arizona:

On January 25, 2012, the state of Arizona became the fourth state to adopt the one-drug protocol. The revised protocol permits execution using either a three-drug or one-drug protocol and requires ADC's director to choose between these two protocols at least seven days prior to a scheduled execution.

Idaho:

In March, 2012, Idaho became the fifth state to adopt the one-drug protocol. This came after a decision by the 9th Circuit Court of Appeals stating that they did not have to make the switch. However, they had difficulties obtaining adequate quantities of the 2nd of the three-drug protocol and thus decided to adopt the one-drug protocol anyway.

Inmates executed using the one-drug method in this state: **1**

Georgia:

On July 17, 2012, Georgia became the sixth state to adopt the one-drug protocol after seeing the success of other states using only the single drug.

Texas:

On July 19, 2012, Texas, leader in U.S. executions, became the seventh state to adopt the one-drug protocol. Without switching to the one-drug protocol, Texas was going to be unable to perform all of the then scheduled executions due to shortages in the 2nd of the three drug protocol.

Inmates executed using the one-drug method in this state: **7**

Other states that have adopted the one-drug protocol, but that have not yet used it:

Arkansas, Kentucky, Louisiana, Missouri, North Carolina, Tennessee

Other States Actions Relating to One-Drug Protocol

California:

In April 2012, California's Governor Jerry Brown ordered prison officials to explore using the one-drug protocol for all future executions. The order came after Marin County Judge D'Opal invalidated the State's regulations after it was discovered that the Department did not follow administrative rules to adopt new guidelines for lethal injection protocols. They failed to adequately review the option of the one-drug protocol, amongst other obligations, and were instructed to follow proper procedures and consider the one-drug option. As of this writing, there is a de-facto moratorium on all executions in California. The abolishment of the death penalty was up for vote in the 2012 session, but failed.

Oregon:

Oregon began consideration of the one-drug protocol as one of its death row prisoners volunteered to forego his appeals and be executed in April 2011, (Haugen v. Premo.) As the date of execution progressed, the Oregon Department of Corrections decided to update its capital punishment guidelines. However, they re-adopted the three-drug protocol without statement as to why they decided against the one-drug alternative. The only statement ODOC has made in rejecting the one-drug argument was to this authors petitions to amend the rules in 2010. Their response then was simply, "The interests of the public and the condemned inmates are best served by denying the petition."

Before the Haugen execution could take place, however, on November 22, 2011 Governor Kitzhaber declared a moratorium on all executions in the state of Oregon, muting the argument for now. The death penalty scheme in Oregon will be reviewed by the Oregon legislature in the 2013 session, at which time one-drug arguments will be added to the conversation.

Virginia:

Emmet v. Johnson, (532 F.3d 291, 7/10/08)

Inmate asserted that Virginia's lethal injection procedures posed an unacceptable risk that the thiopental might not be delivered to him in an amount sufficient to render him unconscious, which would cause him to experience severe pain associated with the administration of the pancuronium bromide and potassium chloride.

Inmate suggested use adoption of the one-drug protocol to cure claims prior to Ohio adoption.

Court found that Virginia was not constitutionally required to eliminate every possibility that pain might occur or every unnecessary risk that may exist. Court affirmed using the Baze standard.

Delaware:

Jackson v. Danberg, (2011 U.S. App. LEXIS 18557, 7/28/11)

8th Amendment argument submitted prior to Ohio adoption. Prisoners favored a one-drug protocol, arguing that maladministration of the three-drug protocol posed a risk of significant pain.

The court held that the plurality opinion in Baze v. Rees controlled the Eighth Amendment method-of-execution challenge. Affirmed using Baze standard.

Court responded, "We recognize that the one-drug protocol is gaining support as an alternative to the three-drug lethal injection protocol, and we commend those states steadily striving to develop more humane alternatives to existing methods of execution. However, federal courts are not "boards of inquiry charged with determining 'best practices' for executions."

Florida:

Valle v. Singer, (2011 U.S. Dist. Lexis 103829, 8/9/11)

8th Amendment argument submitted, suggesting that alternates to the three-drug protocol existed, alluding to the one-drug protocol.

Court ruled that the petitioner "has failed to proffer any alternative procedure or drug, and failed to show that any such alternative procedure or drug is "feasible, readily implemented, and in fact significantly reduce[s] a substantial risk of severe pain.""

Will Other States Switch?

It is noteworthy that in <u>Baze</u> the Court stated at the conclusion of its opinion, "...our approval of a particular method (of execution) in the past has not precluded legislatures from taking the steps they deem appropriate, in light of new developments, to ensure humane capital punishment. There is no reason to suppose that today's decision will be any different." As of the end of 2014, execution protocols are in a flux due to the difficulties in getting the execution drugs of choice and recent botched attempts at killing prisoners with experimental options. It remains to be seen exactly how executions will evolve over the next years. But one thing is certain. There will never be a shortage of condemned prisoners -- or other prisoners for that matter -- who are willing to allow their organs and tissues to be repurposed. There is a will, and a way. The lethal injection protocols are not a roadblock. They are merely a pothole.

WILL DOCTORS EVEN PARTICIPATE?

_____

_____

_____

FACTS:

10

THE NUMBER OF STEPS OF THE LETHAL INJECTION PROCESS BENEFITTED BY PHYSICIAN INVOLVEMENT.

8

THE NUMBER OF STEPS OF THE LETHAL INJECTION PROCESS THAT THE AMA PROHIBITS PHYSICIANS TO PARTICIPATE IN.

41

THE PERCENTAGE OF PHYSICIANS WHO WOULD PARTICIPATE IN THE LETHAL INJECTION PROCESS.

(DESPITE THE AMA'S PROHIBITION.)

CHAPTER 8

Will Physicians Participate?

"FIRST DO NO HARM...

I WILL GIVE NO DEADLY DRUG TO ANY, THOUGH IT BE ASKED OF ME NOR WILL I COUNSEL SUCH."

–HIPPOCRATIC OATH

Due to the above-quoted oath that many physicians take, it has been argued that doctors will not participate in executions. The medical community has been at odds concerning physician participation in the execution process since the inception of capital punishment. It is no surprise that similar conflicts would arise in dealing with the organ donation process in regards to an executed inmate. Therefore, it is important to learn the history of physician involvement in the capital punishment process to determine how to resolve potential ethical dilemmas with our current discussion.

Hippocratic Oath

Physicians belong to an honorable and ethical profession that has been bound by a millenniums old credo. Ask any doctor why he or she does or does not do certain things in certain ways and you'll hear them utter the words "Hippocratic Oath" in almost a kneejerk fashion.

Hippocrates, the father of medicine in western civilization, was a renowned Greek physician, writer and teacher of the 4th century, B.C. The Hippocratic or Coan School (named for Cos, the island he lived on in Greece) that formed around him was of enormous importance in separating medicine from superstitious and philosophical speculation. It placed medicine on a strictly scientific level based on objective observation and critical deductive reasoning. While the Hippocratic Oath cannot directly be attributed to Hippocrates, it undoubtedly represents his ideals and principles.[93]

Many of those opposed to allowing organ donation from executed prisoners still rely primarily on the Hippocratic Oath to forbid physician participation. It is important to note, however, that the Oath, while an extraordinary mantra of health professionals, has never been regarded as an all-inclusive code of behavior. Interpretation of the Oath has been, to some extent, an evolutionary process. In fact, only select parts of the Oath are still being used today, as medicine and ethics have evolved beyond the knowledge of Hippocrates' time. For example, the next sentence of the Oath mentioned above literally reads, "Similarly, I will not give to a woman an abortive remedy."[94]

Thirty years ago, it was contended that performing abortions violated the Hippocratic Oath; today, it claims that assisting in organ donation of condemned inmates does likewise. Clearly, the Hippocratic Oath can have no greater import in deciding this than it did in determining whether women had a constitutional right to have an abortion. In Roe, the Court cited a scholar's conclusion that the Hippocratic Oath "originated in a group representing only a small segment of Greek opinion and that it certainly was not accepted by all ancient physicians." Hippocrates did not face the same ethical and practical questions that medical technology has created for today's physician. The Court stressed the Oath's "rigidity" and was not deterred by its prohibitory language regarding abortion. As Roe shows, a literalist reading of the Hippocratic Oath does not represent the best or final word on medical or legal controversies today.

A literal dissection of the Hippocratic Oath shows that those who take the oath do so by swearing to the pagan gods and goddesses of ancient Greece, thereby binding themselves to mythological deities about whom they know little to nothing about.

Technically, to abide by the oath would mean that those physicians who claim it as their code would be in violation if they subscribed to any Judeo-Christian beliefs or ideas. The oath also directs the doctor to revere his teachers as his parents and to share his money with them (which I guess some doctors may feel as though they're doing so through the years of tuition repayment.) The oath also bars the doctors from instructing the public on matters of personal and public health. No public service announcements (PSAs.)

Were they to adhere to the rigid language of the Oath, not only would doctors be barred from performing abortions or helping terminally ill patients hasten their deaths, but according to a once-accepted interpretation, they would also be prohibited from performing any type of surgery at all. There is a ban on doctor's use of the knife because cutting was considered to be far too crass of a task for the revered status of a physician. That was left to the lower class "barbers" so-called barber-surgeons.

The oath also stipulates dedication to benefitting the sick by staying "free of all intentional injustice, of all mischief, of all sexual relations with both male and female persons." In many ways, the taking of the oath is very much like a priestly vow. Finally, it has a stern warning for those who would breach any aspect of the oath, threatening them with dishonor and infamy "among all men for all time to come."

Many aspects of the oath would now be recognized as preposterous by even the most tradition-bound physicians. Moreover, experience shows that most doctors can and have readily adapted to the changing legal and medical climates. Of the roughly ten main points comprising the Hippocratic Oath, at least seven continue to be violated on a significant scale.

Once the Court held that a woman has a constitutional right to have an abortion, doctors began performing abortions routinely and the ethical integrity of the medical profession remained undiminished. Similarly, doctors would engage in the permitted practice of procuring organs from willing condemned inmates when appropriate, and the integrity of the medical profession would survive without blemish.

The reality – despite many doctors quickness to throw the oath out as their reason for not subscribing to something – is that very few medical schools actually require the oath to be taken by its graduating doctors. That alone renders suspect the hallowed oath's importance or relevance to modern medical practice. Instead of using the Oath as a shield to evade meaningful debate on this controversial issue, the same principles of objective observation and critical deductive reasoning applied by the Oath should provide the best rationale to guide physician's logic on this topic now.

AMA Conflicts

The Hippocratic Oath is not the only excuse that some in the medical profession use to shield them from rational consideration of procuring organs from willing condemned donors. Another common shield is the American Medical Association (AMA). The state has a legitimate interest in assuring the integrity of the medical profession, an interest that includes prohibiting physicians from engaging in conduct that is at odds with their role as healers. Therefore, many states have relied on and implicitly adopted the

AMA's ethical standards into their licensing standards and the AMA has become a powerful entity in the medical field.

In 1980, the AMA formally announced its stance against physician participation in any state-sponsored executions, officially stating that physician participation in executions is grounds for sanctions and license revocation. Further, the AMA stipulated exactly how close physicians can come to an execution before they cross the line into areas that they believe is too far for a doctor to go.[95] In relevant part, these guidelines state:

"Physician participation in execution is defined generally as actions that would fall into one or more of the following categories: (1) an action which would directly cause the death of the condemned; (2) an action which would assist, supervise, or contribute to the ability of another individual to directly cause the death of the condemned; (3) an action which could automatically cause an execution to be carried out on a condemned prisoner."

The AMA further outlines what is and is not considered as "participation" in executions. They cite prohibitions against prescribing medications, monitoring vital signs, rendering technical advice, or attending or observing an execution as a physician; even going so far as to say that the physician can only certify death once the condemned has already been declared to be dead. The only allowances given by the AMA, considered to be non-participatory, are actions strictly testamentary during criminal trials or in a non-professional capacity during the execution.[96]

AMA Declares Organ Donations after Executions Permissible

Despite the fact that the AMA vehemently opposes physician participation in executions, they surprisingly now list organ donation by condemned prisoners as a permissible option, assuming three specific criteria are met.[97]

Organ donation by condemned prisoners is permissible only if:

1) the decision to donate must have been made prior to the inmates conviction,

2) the donated tissue must be removed only after the pronouncement of death and after the body has been removed from the death chamber., and

3) Physicians cannot provide advice on modifying the execution to facilitate organ donation.

- Per American Medical Association Code of Ethics; Opinion E-2.06

The same obstructions, as far as the AMA is concerned, are still in place, but the fact that the AMA approves and provides guidelines regarding organ donation by those executed at all shows the validity of this issue.

Considering the AMA's outspoken opposition on all other aspects of lethal injection, this alone should be seen as a sign of the importance, common sense and necessity of utilizing willing inmates' organs for the benefit of another's survival. But it's not enough to simply look at what a medical society does and does not consider to be taboo when deciding if a medical guideline has merit. Similar to the evolution in medical science and ethics that has rendered the Hippocratic Oath outdated, we have other examples concerning physician participation that guides us on the topic of whether physicians will participate in organ transplantation from condemned inmates.

Historical AMA Conflicts & Physician Participation

Physician-Assisted Suicide

Similar to physician assistance during executions the American Medical Society has prohibited physicians from assisting in hastening the death of those with terminal illnesses. Again, they hold up the Hippocratic Oath "Do no harm" armor, citing and emphasizing that by any involvement in a patients' death a physician risks the integrity of the medical community.

In an amicus brief filed in a key assisted-suicide case,[98] the AMA attached a Journal of American Medicine article, reporting the conclusion of the AMA's Council on Ethical and Judicial Affairs on assisted suicide. The article concluded, "The societal risk of involving physicians in medical interventions to cause patients' death is too great in this culture to condone euthanasia or physician-assisted suicide at this time."

The arguers of that case responded, "The assertion that following the wishes of an already dying patient will erode the commitment of doctors to help their patients rests both on an ignorance of what numbers of doctors have been doing for a considerable time and on a misunderstanding of the proper function of a physician." They argued that doctors have been discreetly helping terminally ill patients hasten their deaths for decades and probably centuries, while acknowledging privately that there was no other medical purpose to their actions. "They have done so with the tacit approval of a substantial percentage of both the public and the medical profession, and without in any way diluting their commitment to their patients."

In addition, doctors have been able to openly take actions that will result in the deaths of their patients. They may terminate life-support systems, withdraw life-sustaining gastronomy tubes, otherwise terminate or withhold all other forms of medical treatment and may even administer lethal doses of drugs with full knowledge of their "double effect", or in some states, openly satisfy the patients' willingness to die. Given the similarity between what doctors are now permitted to do and what opponents asserted they should be permitted to do, there is no risk at all to the integrity of the profession. This is a conclusion that is shared by a growing number of doctors who openly support issues such as physician-assisted suicide and proclaim it fully compatible with the physicians' calling and with their commitment and obligation to help the sick. According to a survey by the American Society of Internal Medicine, one doctor in five said he had already assisted in a patients' suicide, without such legal backing.[99]

In assisted suicide, whether or not a patient can be cured, the doctor has an obligation to attempt to alleviate his pain and suffering. If it is impossible to cure the patient or retard the advance of his disease, then the doctor's primary duty is to make the patient as comfortable as possible. When performing that task, the doctor is performing a proper medical function, even though he knows that his patients' death is a necessary and inevitable consequence of his actions.

Recognizing the right to "assisted–suicide" did not require doctors to do anything contrary to their individual principles. A physician whose moral or religious beliefs would prevent him from assisting a patient to hasten his death is free to follow the dictates of his conscience. Those doctors who believe that terminally ill, competent, adult patients should be permitted to choose the time and manner of their death are able to help them do so. Extending a choice to doctors as well as to patients has helped protect the integrity of the medical profession without compromising the rights or principles of individual doctors and without sacrificing the welfare of their patients.

Physician Participation in Executions Now

The same extension of choice is true of physician participation in capital punishment. The first line of the AMA code of ethics regarding this topic states, "An individual's opinion on capital punishment is the personal moral decision of the individual." However, the AMA goes on to state specifically, "A physician, as a member of a profession dedicated to preserving life when there is hope of doing so, should not be a participant in a legally authorized execution." So much for freedom of moral choice.

While a doctor should not be a participant in an execution, according to the AMA, there is no hope of preserving life in the case of the execution. At the moment when all appeals and petitions for clemency have been turned down and the condemned is strapped down to the gurney, the man is condemned to death by execution in a way where he cannot escape his fate. In thinking practically, the man facing imminent execution has no more hope of recovery than a terminally ill or even a brain dead patient.

Even taking the AMA's code as its intended though, there are numerous examples of physicians who participate in state-administered executions. Some physicians argue that because there is no doctor-patient relationship between the condemned inmate and the physician participation in the execution, assisting in the execution does not violate any of the medical ethics. This is assuming that it is not the prisons doctor who is participating. Some physicians feel that they have a duty to serve their country, comparing their participation to other civic duties like serving on a jury, voting or soldiering in a time of war.

Whatever the reasoning, physicians have taken part in executions since the inception of capital punishment as well as beyond the AMA's resolutions against it. Nearly all capital punishment statutes refer to the presence of a physician in some fashion undoubtedly for the reasons of their expertise. While not wanting to step on the toes of the AMA or other medical societies, legislatures may phrase the statute as "shall" attend while assigning no official duties. However, the sensible reason is obvious. Additionally, several states have advanced laws that specify that no negative repercussions are to come to a medical professional who assists in an execution. [100]

This is further demonstrated by the proposed federal governments rule establishing lethal injection as the method of execution. The proposed rule required the presence of a physician during all federal executions. Due to the opposition of the AMA, numerous calls and letters in opposition to the proposed rule flooded the Justice Department. After reviewing the resistance, the final rule eliminated the requirement of physician attendance. However, the rule did not prohibit physician attendance. According to the federal regulation, "Because the Department may conclude that a physician's presence is necessary to a responsible execution, physician participation will not be barred."[101] Moreover, the final codification simply left it up to the Wardens discretion stating that the 'Warden may grant access to anyone deemed necessary'.[102]

Regardless of these kinds of debates and the stance of medical societies, physicians do participate in lethal injections. In 2001, a cross-sectional survey of 413 practicing physicians showed that 41% of the respondents were willing to perform at least one action involving capital punishment that was disallowed by the AMA.[103] Those who chose to go against the AMA's guidelines ranged from the 19% who were willing to administer the lethal chemicals to the 36% who were willing to determine death.[104] As a renowned Harvard Professor of Anesthesiology stated, "Because the potential benefits are sufficiently clear and the potential harms are poorly explicated, we should permit physician participation in capital punishment."[105]

Doctors Will Participate

While the AMA vehemently opposes physician assistance in capital executions, the AMA is not a governing body, and it does not possess the power to either sanction or discipline physicians who choose to ignore its policies. That power is reserved to state licensing boards for physicians, which are instruments of the government. While the AMA is a powerful entity in the medical community, it has been struggling to maintain its physician membership. Early in the 20th century, nine in ten doctors were members. Today, with about 250,000 members, that number is fewer than one in three, and some estimates are lower. Membership is, after all, voluntary; not compulsory.

There is obviously a pull away from the AMA's importance in medical matters and, as has been demonstrated, there is a clear lack of consensus between individual doctors and the AMA. It is no doubt that this lack of consensus will carry over to the issue of physician participation in organ donation from an executed inmate.

In some cases the facts that lives are being saved will potentially serve to assuage some concern over participation. However, based on the history of physicians' willingness to participate in other equally controversial issues, there will likely be little difficulty in obtaining the participation of doctors to assist in the processes involving organ donations from the condemned. In fact, some have already stepped forward to offer their assistance.

However, we have still not exhausted all of the concerns. What remains are philosophical conflicts, or in other words, the fear of the 'what-ifs'. As these are oftentimes rooted in a very sincere place within the individual raising the concerns, it is important that we address them.

PART THREE

Prisoner Organ Donation – Other Concerns

With the primary concerns preventing prisoner organ donation clarified, it is hoped that the transplant community and prisons will begin taking the careful steps towards allowing such donations to take place. However, as with any controversial topic, oftentimes reason and rationality are forced to pause to make way for other less tangible concerns.

There are those who specialize in thinking things through beyond the obvious benefits. Known as ethicists, these are paid to determine not whether things can happen, but whether or not they should happen. The stigma of prison and controversy itself causes ethicists to be torn on the issue of organ donation from prisoners. Because these ethicists are the equivalent of a moral fiber and a barometer on whether or not society will be accepting of this controversial topic, the transplant industry is especially careful to listen to what these ethicists have to say on the topic. Therefore, it must be considered here.

Organ transplantation itself has a relatively short history that was fraught with complications and ethical concerns throughout. There are some who strongly felt that organ donation itself was morally wrong and should not be allowed. It is important to look at that history and to see how the transplant community evolved into what it is today and how vital it is that it continues evolving to allow for donations from healthy willing prisoners today.

It is unfortunate, but even Hollywood can have an adverse impact on whether organ donations from prisoners occur.. Thanks to

Hollywood's portrayal of organ transplants gone wrong, there is a fear that the prisoner may "live on" through their donated parts in the body of the unsuspecting recipient and perpetuate the bad that caused that person to be a criminal in the first place. As ridiculous as it may sound, there have actually been studies performed to look into this, with some surprising findings. Because this, as well as ethical issues and other concerns affect organ donation from prisoners directly, these are topics worthy of consideration.

CHAPTER 9

Is Prisoner Organ Donation Ethical?

"ORGAN DONATION FROM DEAD PATIENTS WILL ALWAYS BE A SENSITIVE MORAL ENTERPRISE. WE MUST NOT RISK ETHICALLY SULLYING THIS PRACTICE BY HARVESTING ORGANS FROM EXECUTED PRISONERS."

–Kenneth Prager
Professor of clinical medicine
Columbia College of Physicians and Surgeons

"REGARDLESS OF YOUR POSITION ON CAPITAL PUNISHMENT, THESE EXECUTIONS DO OCCUR AND VIABLE ORGANS ARE WASTED...FACILITATING ORGAN DONATIONS FROM DEATH ROW PRISONERS CLEARLY SERVES THE PUBLIC GOOD."

–Marrick Kukin
Professor of clinical medicine
Columbia College of Physicians and Surgeons

The above-quoted professionals were cited earlier to demonstrate the disparity of opinions on the topic of organ and tissue donation from death row inmates. In case you didn't catch it before, though, I wanted to point a few things out. What may be most obvious, apart from their opposing stance on the issue, is that these two physicians hold identical positions. Not only do they hold the same title, they work in the same hospital, likely seeing each other more than they want to every working day of their lives. Both of their quotes came from New York Times 'Letters to the Editor' that were published in response to the Times article I wrote concerning my wish to donate organs from death row. It turned out that these two doctors are friends. They go to the same synagogue. Maybe their kids play together. Neither doctor even knew the other had penned a letter to the editor, which conjures thoughts of them reading that days Times while at their desks, peeking across the hall to see if their colleague had gotten to that page yet. They eventually noticed each had been published with opposing viewpoints and debated the topic, essentially agreeing to disagree. But for us, they've became a glaring example of how strong opinions reside on both sides of the fence on the issue of prisoner organ donation.

The reason for such bi-polar opinions from experts has little to do with whether prisoner organ donation can happen. Most agree that it is doable, once some logistical issue gat hammered out. And it's not a matter of whether donations from inmates would save lives. That's apparent. Rather, it is largely due to the ethical interpretations on each side, whether it should happen. As our antagonist above stated, "We must not risk ethically sullying this practice..."

'Ethics' is the dirty word by which many things that sound practical get stomped on before they can become a reality. Since we're debating with the lives of those who will die without a needed organ, the opinions on ethics cannot be taken lightly.

The other extreme comes from the side filled with those who actually need the organs or tissue to survive. Drop by any hospital or dialysis clinic and approach anyone in need of an organ, and it will be evident that nearly everyone who is not considering it from a strictly ethical standpoint is on the side that agrees with prisoner organ donation. While many will object to someone being tied down, dropped into a tub of ice and having a kidney forcefully liberated from their body to provide the part they need, you can't exactly rely on them to give an unbiased answer as to whether something is ethically a good idea.

So were left with professionals who can't agree whether something is ethical or not and those who have far too many horses in the race of their life to provide the reasonable answer.

Perhaps a balance should be to consider what the public thinks, because without their general support we might as well stop talking about it now. It seems that that's how most ethical discussions are hashed out anyway, in the court of public opinion. But if the public is overwhelmingly in support of these donations, where are we? We'll stand with millions for it on one side, and some highly respected officials and ethicists against it on the other. It doesn't get us any closer to solving the dilemma, ethically or otherwise.

"Ethics" are a funny thing because they don't come with a set manual. In fact, if you try to find such a manual, you'll discover an entire section of a library containing seemingly endless philosophies on the subject. Even though by definition ethics are moral principles that govern a group's behavior, there are no absolute criteria to guide to a solution. Beyond the obvious things that we all know to be right and wrong from infancy, ethics govern the shades-of-gray middle ground. They are defined as the "reflective study of what is good or bad in that part of human conduct for which man has some personal responsibility."[106] Some will argue them from a religious or emotional standpoint, while another will argue it from a strictly utilitarian point of view. Therefore, unfortunately, it makes for a very subjective field that will never be satisfied for all involved.

As with any subjective argument, the opposing points of view become polarizing extremes that require a compromise, or else everyone loses. Ethicists will recognize this as Aristotle's 'doctrine of the mean' (mesotes).[107] However, when lives are weighing in the balance – as is the case with organ donations – it's vital that the topic is carefully considered immediately before more lives are lost.

"Experts" vs. Public Opinion

The public agrees that organ donations from prisoners should be allowed. Polls on the GAVE Prisoner Organ Donation advocacy website have consistently shown that well over 85% of those who come onto the site click the 'Yes' option where asked if prisoners should be allowed to be organ and tissue donors. But seeing as how the visitors to the site generally arrive with an pre-conceived interest in the topic already, it's likely not really an unbiased poll. As yet, there has been no Gallup-type poll, or even one that calls households to catch people off-guard right as dinner's about to be served to convince them to take an unbiased survey. However, the media has polled the people and the people are overwhelmingly in favor of prisoner organ donation. Here are a few examples:

"Should Prisoners be Allowed to Donate Organs and Tissue?"
NBC.com (2013 -- 87,316 polled): Yes: 77%; No: 15%; Undecided: 8%[108]

Regional (Oregon) Polls
Statesman Journal: Yes: 65.4%, No: 23.3%, Don't Know: 7%[109]
KATU2 News: Yes: 76.5%, No: 17%, Don't Know: 6.5%[110]

When digging a little deeper into the thoughts of those who took the polls, or reading their comments posted under the above-mentioned polls, you find that many are surprised to find out that such donations were not already allowed and being performed. When it comes to the topic of organ donations from those who are executed, a common sentiment is, 'It seems absurd that the state has no qualms about executions, but do they really feel that letting a condemned man donate his soon-to-be-otherwise-useless organs is crossing some ethical line?'

Occasionally somebody crops up on the comment boards to state an objection such as, 'You can't be certain why an inmate is donating.'

But the rational one's quickly bombard with comments that when it's a life, or several innocent lives that are weighing in the balance, it doesn't really matter why an inmate is asking to donate. "Who are we to judge motivations anyway? Why does anyone sign up to be donors?"[111] some have asked.

Most practical thinkers see it as a simple math equation. Somebody needs an organ and somebody wants to give them one. Why does it matter where the organs come from so long as they're healthy and given willingly?

However, then come the ethical volleys from the other side of the net, from the smaller but more powerful team. "Experts" from every field weigh in. While many professionals in the transplant field stay on the popular side and offer support, others stand in opposition of prisoner organ donation, citing those subjective "ethical" restrictions. In addition, with the death penalty in the picture, you get anti–death penalty groups stepping up to interject and complicate the matter further. Moreover, because you're dealing with a medical issue, bioethics come into play to guarantee that it becomes as complicated as the issues of abortion or euthanasia, threatening to extend the debate for years. It can become so convoluted that many experts take the advice, "the best way to solve an ethical dilemma is to avoid being put in that situation in the first place," as stated by ethicist Edward Hundert – published in the Harvard Guide on Psychiatry on ethical issues.[112]

Through quotes from "experts" in their fields, the conflicts are clear.

On the topic of prisoner "consent":

"I don't think we want to be the kind of society that takes organs from prisoners. To do so would be to use unfree prisoners as a means to an end."

-Paul R. Heft
Director of the Charles Warren Fairbanks Center for Medical Ethics

"Organ donation from prisoners raises significant ethical issues about the ability of prisoners to provide coercion-free consent."

- Alexandra Glazier
Head of UNOS Ethics Committee

"It's impossible to be sure that a person behind bars is making a decision they would make while walking down the street."

-Jeffrey Orlowski
Executive Director of the Association of Organ Procurement Organizations

"In a prison situation, there's not a lot of freedom of choice for that individual. It's hard to tell if this person is making a choice, or are they just doing this to get some sort of reward or avoid further punishment."

-Joel Newman
Spokesman for United Network for Organ Sharing

Those consent arguments should sound familiar from chapter five. However, experts use these as "ethical" arguments as well. To reiterate my response to these arguments: If a prisoner makes an unsolicited decision to donate an organ, meets stringent criteria, is given no incentive to do so, and gives the same consent that current laws dictate for organ donors and for other invasive procedures, his voluntary choice to donate is absolute and clear.

Some ethical concerns that we haven't yet discussed:

Organ donation from executed inmates:

"Allowing condemned prisoners to donate organs could provide an inappropriate incentive to execute prisoners and lead to significant human rights violations. Any possibility that particular groups or individuals could receive death sentences to provide transplantable parts to the public would be completely objectionable."

- Alexandra Glazier
Head of UNOS Ethics Committee

"A court might not want to delay an execution if it meant a person is going to die."

-Richard Dieter
Executive Director of Death Penalty Information Center

"If you make it possible for death row inmates to donate organs, then the state has a vested interest in death sentences. So, the number of death sentences may increase because of that, which is a major judicial and ethical issue."

-
Richard Brittingham, MD, Lawton

"Society should not be twisted in a utilitarian direction so (a prisoner) can assuage his guilt or give his life purpose. If we ever start killing people for their organs, we will have opened a Pandora's box that will never close."

-Wesley J. Smith
Senior Fellow at Discovery Institutes Center on Human Exceptionalism

"If this lifesaving is allowed to come out of death, it will only lead to more death, as capital punishment is rationalized away as 'something not so bad'."

-Mansfield Frazier
Executive Director of Neighborhood Solutions

"Whatever you think of the death penalty, allowing an executed prisoner to redeem himself by organ donation completely undermines the rationale for execution by turning murderers' into heroes."

-Arthur Caplan
Ethicist, University of Pennsylvania, Department of Medical Ethics

A brief response to these, because I can't help it. The transplant community has ensured that organ donations are given anonymously. No prisoner will be made a "hero" publicly. Whatever the donor thinks of himself, or if he's doing it for redemptive reasons, so be it. He'll be gone tomorrow, while the innocent recipient, who would have died otherwise, will get to live for decades longer. Does it really matter if the condemned prisoner feels something positive in his last few moments alive at the expense of several other innocent lives?

Most assumed that prisoners could donate organs already. Therefore, to argue that it will cause an influx of death sentences or court interventions is unreasonable.

Compromise?

There is a general theme that is common in all ethical conversations and can be seen from the preceding quotes. "What if?" Many refer to it as that "slippery slope" argument (also known as 'the camel's nose under the tent', 'a foot in the door', and 'give an inch take a mile'.). Every time the catchphrase appears, it implies eventual moral disaster through supposedly inevitable abuse of a "radical" change, no matter how small or innocuous its beginning. Or, in other words, by allowing this to happen, disaster is imminent, therefore, we cannot allow it to happen. Another shield.

Similar arguments have come up in every medical controversy. Those opposed to physician–assisted suicide said that opening the door to euthanasia would lead to an expansion of assisted suicide beyond the terminally ill and mentally competent.[113] Anti–abortionists raised similar concerns of abuses. Consider, for example, birth control. In the opening decades of the 20th Century, the law declared the practice of birth control to be immoral, thus unethical, and therefore illegal. Margaret Sanger, an outspoken nurse in 1910, strongly disagreed and went on a campaign to try to force the issue on the ethicists of the day. The ethically pious medical experts didn't debate the topic, or even just declare birth control to be unethical. Instead, they persecuted its most outspoken proponent with gusto and voluntarily helped authorities to imprison her so that she could not continue fighting for it. It wasn't until 1937 that the misguided experts came to their senses to certify birth control as a legitimate medical service, shortly after Ms. Sanger authored a book on the topic[114] – a powerful motivation for this very publication.

Even with living donations, where a living donor allows a kidney or part of their liver to be taken from him to gift to someone else in need, ethicists sounded the alarm announcing their opposition to the idea. You may recall Dr. Murray, who performed the first successful living kidney transplant. The doctor and the twin brothers who volunteered for the transplant faced a mountain of criticism from the medical community, stating that it was unethical to operate on healthy humans. Respected ethicists and editors of medical journals wrote that it was contrary to the Hippocratic Oath's vow to never do harm to anyone, vehemently opposing the transplant. Yet, this transplant ended up winning Dr. Murray a Nobel Prize for what the transplant did for the future of transplantation. Now with prisoner organ donations, ethicists are again sounding the alarm, this time that there will come a tide of prisoners' abuses, consent issues, juries sentencing more people to death, or something similar to China's horrible practices.

The 'what if?' issues certainly cannot be ignored. A lot of time and effort has gone into exploring many of those in these chapters. Likewise, however, the possibilities cannot be ignored. To sit behind a barricade of subjective ethics and say that this is impossible, without doing the research, is – at the least – unfair to those whose lives could be saved. A one-time president of the Commission for the Study of Ethical Problems in Medicine concluded the point most eloquently.

"Much more is needed that merely pointing out that allowing one kind of action (itself justified) could conceivably increase the tendency to allow another action (unjustified). Rather, it must be shown that pressures to allow the unjustified action will become so strong once the initial step is taken that the further steps are likely to occur... (and) such evidence is commonly quite limited."[115]

When an issue is raised that a majority of the public agree with, especially if there is no law in the land against it, it seems obvious to implement it as a permitted practice. There is no law preventing prisoners from donating their organs. However, when the opposition is the gatekeeper – as is the case here – nothing can happen without an outcry that changes their ethical hang-ups.

One last quote perhaps says it best. In response to the ethical notions that accepting executed prisoners organs would be an incentive for juries and judges to impose capital punishment, she said:

"It's an absurd and morbid fantasy. This is just the kind of outlandish scare tactic people use when they have no rational arguments against the issue."

- Sally Satel
Psychiatrist and Scholar at the American Enterprise Institute

Those in need of organs, those prisoners who want to donate, and the public are on one island. The transplant community (in part), the prisons, and some ethicists are on another island on this issue. Yet, a bridge can be built between the two. With lives at stake, these extremes require a compromise. Most ethicists will agree with the need to find a 'mean' between extremes. But some ethicists will argue that this is one of those novel occasions where such a compromise won't work. However, a reasonable balance can be made that satisfies even the most squeamish concern.

When we're dealing with medical issues, a "compromise" usually translates into a great set of safeguards. For instance, most ethicists put down their sirens concerning the issue of living organ donations when the proper safeguards were laid out to ensure the appropriate consent of all involved parties. There is no law against organ donation from prisoners and, in fact, some medical associations do set guidelines for donations from the executed as seen in previous chapters.[116] Nevertheless, specific protocols and guidelines are necessary to ensure that none of the feared abuses takes place.

It so happens that prisons are experts at constructing rules for both the staff and prisoners to follow. With the extent of litigation that has taken place in the system, they have to be. Prisons also have an obligation to maintain positive community relationships and typically do so through inmate programs and services. As one common prison rule states, "A continuous effort will be made to balance statewide system interests with local community needs."[117] What better community effect can be had than the literal saving of lives?

The other half of the equation for setting necessary safeguards is the transplant community. As with most medical fields, they are supremely cautious. They have careful and strict safeguards to ensure that the interests of both the one who needs an organ and the donor are met. Their mission is perpetually to increase the supply of healthy donated organs. But they do so with a Fabian approach, like walking on eggshells in an abundance of deliberate carefulness. It's this industry that put a stop to donations from prisoners' decades ago, at the advent of AIDS. They're so cautious that – as learned in chapter two – they've continued this ban even though now proper modern testing can rule out dangers of disease transmission. The point is, though, that they are great at constructing careful guidelines to make certain that all involved benefit and are protected.

Together, the prison system and the transplant community can make this happen. With safeguards to ensure appropriate consent and to end disease transmission, inmate donations are ethical and safe. With courage from the transplant authorities and prison directors to evolve beyond the perceived social taboos, we may just find that healthy, voluntary prisoners are what we needed to stem the advancing tidal wave of organ shortages in the U.S.

They can overcome the antiquated ideas and misconceptions to develop a method by which willing prisoners who are healthy can donate to those in need.

The AMA Code of Medical Ethics plainly states, "A physician shall recognize a responsibility to participate in activities contributing to an improved community."[118] To dismiss a concept that can absolutely benefit a group of people with a group who is willing to assist simply out of possible ethical 'what-if' fear denies an opportunity to fix a, thus far, unfixable problem in the U.S. The alternatives exist right now. As the 20th Century's most prolific and best-known ethicist John Dewey himself reasoned, 'An intelligent and serious inquiry is required to come up with a judgment and choice concerning a given situation. These are to be the best that can be made in view of the predictable consequences of the proposed action.'[119] To not give it more than a waving of the hand holding an ethical flag is an injustice and a tragedy. Even the fear of abuse can be (and often is) abused.

With lives literally being lost in the process – another one in the time it took to read this chapter – it should weigh heavily on the minds and consciences of anyone who raises an outdated "ethical" roadblock.

But I'm an inmate. Who am I to second-guess the wisdom of the experts? Okay, I'll leave the chapter with one final quote that perhaps best sums up the ethical arguments. As the legal scholar, Richard Epstein has put it:

"Only a bioethicist could prefer a world in which we have 1,000 altruists per annum and over 6,500 excess deaths over one in which we have no altruists and no excess deaths."

CHAPTER 10

But They Are the Experts

"THE FUNCTION OF THE EXPERTS IS NOT TO BE MORE RIGHT THAN OTHERS, BUT TO BE WRONG FOR MORE SOPHISTICATED REASONS."

-David Butler, British psephologist

It is awkward to stand in the shadow of the transplant policy-makers and tell them that they are wrong. Being a prisoner who has made some of the most horrendous decisions a human can make, I shouldn't be able to stand up to such an entity, much less hope to influence something are completely focused on. It's not David versus Goliath. It's that little beetle that Goliath's shield carrier almost crushed on the way to fight David, versus Goliath's bigger brother – UNOS and the government's Organ Procurement and Transplantation Network (OPTN.) If this were one of those issues that I was passionate about, but that the rest of normal society decided was way off base, I would likely acquiesce and figure that one of my screws could use a handyman with a Phillips-head driver in his belt to do a little tightening. But you've seen the numbers. Seventy-seven percent of the tens of thousands polled are on my side, including some in the transplant field. A distinct minority agree with the transplant policy-makers. Suddenly I feel tall for a beetle.

Since I've been paying such closer attention to field of transplantation, it has become apparent that this isn't the only issue where numbers have sided against the transplant community to force them to change their policies. Here are just a few of the recent high profile examples.

A Little Girls Lungs

Sarah Murnaghan needed lungs. Without them she would die. She had been hospitalized for months with end-stage cystic fibrosis while hoping two lungs would be found to let her live life as fully as the rest of her body would let her. She made it to the top of the transplant list just in time, but no lungs were available – at least not from another child. National transplant policy left no choice but to put her at the bottom of the list for adult lungs – behind patients who were far less critically ill. She would not make it.

It wasn't as though their weren't lungs available that would fit. This wasn't a size matter. Years earlier the transplant professionals had perfected the ability to custom fit adult-sized lungs into a child's body. But the transplant authorities never adjusted the rules to allow for children to be treated equally in lung allocation policies. For over a decade, if a child needed lungs they would have to get them from another child. If that couldn't be accomplished, then they would stand in the futile line behind an interminably long queue of people much bigger than them. It's just the way it was. It was the rule and, as Sarah's parents quickly found out, the rule was unbendable.

Left with no other options but to be outraged, Sarah's parents filed suit to change national lung allocation rules to reflect modern advances. They immediately began a courtship with the national media, as if their lives depended on it. They shouted from every rooftop with a broadcast tower they could find. They invited CNN into Sarah's hospital room to show the world who the policy-makers were fighting. The transplant policy-makers absolutely fought back, airing on the same news channels, trying to convince the world that to allow this would topple the system and cause much greater loss of life. They argued in court that, while the loss of this little girl's life would be tragic, the unintended consequences of adjusting the policy would be more so. The system in place worked and should not be changed. The federal judge hearing the case disagreed and intervened, forcing OPTN to add Sarah towards the top of the adult list.

The action spurred a national debate and brought the health experts and medical ethicists out of their dens. Was this the right thing to do? Did the judge just sign the death sentences of countless adults who would be shoved aside for younger models? In the meantime, Sarah got her lungs just in time. She survived. Another in a similar circumstance in her same hospital now has a chance at life that he would not likely have had otherwise. Not one story surfaced of any adult who was unable to get a lifesaving pair of lungs because of this forced change in protocol. However, if Sarah's parents simply accepted the outdated rules and remained quiet as their daughter died, we would not have heard of her either, nor the uncountable children who would have faced a similar fate without this long overdue change in policy.

The Bone Marrow Compensation Debate

In 1984, Congress passed the National Organ Transplant Act banning the purchase or sale of organs like livers and lungs for transplants. The intention was, and continues to be, to prevent the exploitation of poor donors - similar to the idea discussed earlier of exploitation of prisoners. If you don't offer incentives to donate, abuse is less likely. Swept up in that ban were bone marrow donations, which remained in effect until just recently. The transplant community was, and of this writing still is, livid.

Efforts to challenge the ban on compensating bone marrow donors began in 2009, led by the Institute for Justice, a public interest law firm. The firm's clients, initially Doreen Flynn -- whose three children have a rare disease called Franconia anemia - then later joiners to the suit, dozens of families, were all afraid their ill loved ones would die because they couldn't get a transplant. What they knew that general society wasn't all that familiar with was that technology had long ago surpassed the original reason that bone marrow was included in that 1984 ban. There was now no reason to ban compensation. It no longer made sense to continue this ban when they needed all the donors they could get. To them, even one more registered donor increased the likelihood that their loved ones would survive. To allow compensation for bone marrow would increase the size of the donor pool dramatically, and could mean the difference between life and death.

Bone marrow is the body's blood manufacturing factory. For some sick patients, such as patients with leukemia, the only way to save their lives is to kill the cancer cells in their blood., which they do so through chemotherapy or radiation. The treatments kill the white blood cells essential to their immune systems. But since these cells are needed for survival, they must be replaced quickly with healthy cells. Further, they must be replaced with the stem cells, which mature into the needed white blood cells. The only way to get these stem cells is through bone marrow transplants.

Until about twenty years ago, bone marrow was extracted from donor's bones by "aspiration." This is the method that most of us assumed was still taking place. Long scary needles, thick enough to suck out the soft, fatty bone marrow, were inserted right into the hipbone of the donor. The thick hipbone is a good reservoir for marrow, but it's also a painful and invasive place for the donor to be stabbed, requiring hospitalization.

In the mid-90s, however, new technology superseded this technique. With this newer method, called "apheresis," now used in at least two-thirds of bone marrow transplants, none of the soft fatty variety of marrow is actually needed, therefore no more hip-stabbing. Sick patients don't need everything that the soft marrow provided from the actual bone, just some of the marrow's stem cells. Most stem cells stay in the bone marrow cavity and grow into mature blood cells there, before passing into the blood vessels. But some blood stem cells flow and circulate through the bloodstream before they mature. Through the process of apheresis, these blood stem cells are extracted in a similar method as with blood donations, with no need for sedatives or anesthesia, through a needle inserted into the donor's vein. Blood is withdrawn from the vein and filtered through an apheresis machine to extract the necessary cells, with the remaining components of the blood being returned to the donor's vein. The extracted stem blood cells are replaced by the donor's bone marrow in three to six weeks as if nothing happened. Lives are saved. Complications are exceedingly rare.

The main difference between an ordinary blood donation and apheresis is that instead of just filling up a plastic bag with whole blood, the donor sits for some hours in a recliner while the blood passes through the apheresis machine. This same apheresis technique is sometimes used for purposes other than bone marrow donations, such as when the machine is set up to collect plasma or platelets, rather than stem cells, from a donor's blood. When it is used for these other purposes, the identical technique is called a "blood donation" or "blood plasma donation." For these, the transplant industry condones compensation for the donor. However, when used to separate out and collect the stem cells from the donor's bloodstream, apheresis is called "peripheral blood stem cell apheresis" or a "bone marrow donation," which, antithetically, the transplant community opposes any payment for.

In December of 2012, the U.S. Court of Appeals for the Ninth Circuit took the side of the families that filed suit to change the ban, ruling unanimously in their favor. With this ruling having the potential to markedly increase donors, this would seem like a win for the entire transplant community. But the those who make all of the decisions in the transplant community, the very ones that are so vocally against donations from prisoners, are beside themselves with outrage. After the ruling came down, and upon finding out the Attorney General was not going to seek Supreme Court review, The National Bone Marrow Donor Program (NMDP), one of the decision-makers, issued this statement. "Paying marrow donors creates a multitude of problems and will not help more patients receive transplants. Compensation will limit treatment options for patients, decrease the quality of donations, and divert much-needed money from areas where it can help a wider range of patients. Research in the blood community has shown that paid blood donors are more likely to have infectious diseases than are unpaid donors." You get a little déjà-vu when you read that after considering what we have thus far about inmate donations. The go-to scare tactic of the opposed policy-makers is the infectious disease card, which we know can be now screened properly.

Not being able to defeat the ruling, the concluding statement on the issue came from Michael Boo, chief strategy officer with the NMDP and BetheMatch, the national bone marrow donor registry, was, "Our policy has always been to operate a directory of all volunteers. We will not list donors that have been promised compensation." That same policy has also since been adopted by HRSA, the government ruler of all things transplant related. To this day, they will not list donors who have been promised compensation and they are actively trying to get Congress to amend the law to specifically prohibit compensating apheresis donors. The Department of Health and Human Services is proposing a rule-making action that seeks to override the court's decision by redefining marrow extracted from the bloodstream as an "organ."

To be fair and to tell it from their perspective, the registry has grown substantially over the years without the need for compensation. For those on the list waiting for a donor, they feel that the problem is not an issue of inadequate volunteer donor numbers, but rather the rarity of the patient's particular genetic make-up. If this is the case, they do not believe that compensating donors will solve the problem. What has begun to make inroads in solving this problem, in their view, is the funding of science that has come up with alternative treatments.

None of their arguments stands up to scrutiny. While this research is necessary and has offered advances that have helped find options for many of those in need, we come back to simple math. More donors equals more lives saved, even of those with those rare genetic make-ups. If that were not the case, BeTheMatch and the very claimants who say that compensation is not necessary would not be actively trying to find ways to register more donors. One stop at their website, or happening upon one of their television, radio, or online marketing spots will prove that even they see the need to continue increasing the bone marrow donor pool. Should we ban compensation for blood donations because science has found other ways help those who previously needed blood, or because the shortage is especially extreme in hard to find blood types?

If banning donor compensation encouraged a satisfactory amount of altruistic donations, it would already have done so. The ban has been in place for decades and the result is chronic bone-marrow shortages. The system in place in not working. Adding the element of compensation for this renewable resource, a system that has been working well in the U.S. for blood, sperm and egg donations, may be part of the answer in finally solving the bone marrow shortage in this country.

Discarded Kidneys

As of June 2013, 96,635 patients are waiting in line on transplant lists to receive a kidney. About 17,000 will be fortunate enough to get them this year. Around 5,000 will not be so fortunate and will die waiting. The rest will have to continue waiting. But a disastrous reality that most of us are not aware of is that half of those who didn't make it likely may have died because the kidney that could have saved their life was thrown out. As a September 2012 New York Times cover story related, "Last year 4,720 people died while waiting for kidney transplants in the United States. And yet, as in each of the last five years, more than 2,600 kidneys were recovered from deceased donors and then discarded without being transplanted, government data show." The reason for such a waste? The rules established by the experts at OPTN and UNOS.

According to these experts, the system is simple and transparent. However, many in the transplant field argue that the current system wastes precious opportunities for transplants. One recent computer simulation, by researchers with the Scientific Registry of Transplant Recipients, projected that a redesigned system could add 10,000 years of life from just one year of transplants. The current kidney matching system does not consider factors such as the projected life expectancy of the recipient, or even the urgency of the transplant. Whereas, the systems for allocating livers, hearts, and lungs have been revised to weigh those aspects. Kidneys account for more then three-quarters of the national organ waiting lists, yet they are allocated under the oldest set of guidelines that govern organ distribution.

Scenario: An elderly patient waits at the top of the kidney transplant list for a kidney because the system in place does not discriminate by age or projected life span. Because the patient is at the top of the list and kidneys become available with greater frequency, he can afford to pass on an okay but older, lower-quality kidney that shows up. Instead, he can hold out for a young healthy kidney that has decades of life left in it. If the okay kidney is passed up too often, doctors say, a kidney can develop a self-fulfilling reputation as an unwanted organ. The okay organ, still able to provide life, ends up in the trash, unable to find a taker. It's like putting the last new set of tires on the car with a sputtering engine when the car with low miles is left to sit and collect rust and die because he mistakenly heard the spares were flat.

Take Judith Kurash, who died at the age of 72 after suffering a brain aneurism. Surgeons successfully transplanted her liver. Her heart went to research. But because of Ms. Kurash's age and history of hypertension, her kidneys had trouble finding a home. They were turned down by five area hospitals, six Midwestern ones and then 37 others nationwide, before finally being accepted by a center on the East Coast. By the time the kidneys arrived at the East Coast for transplant, the left one was viable and transplanted. However, the right one had "timed out" and was tossed in the trash.

More than half of the discarded organs come from older donors like Ms. Kurash, whose age and health problems made them marginal for transplant. But in 2011, nearly 1,000 of the discarded kidneys came from donors who were younger than 60, according to UNOS. Certainly some of the kidneys were truly unsuitable for transplantation. But some authorities, like Dr. Barry M. Straube, who served for six years as Medicare's chief medical officer, and Dr. Robert J. Stratta, the director of transplantation at Wake Forest School of Medicine, speculate that as many as half of discarded kidneys could be transplanted. While there are factors that come in to play to cause doctors to pass up on marginal kidneys, the biggest problem has been that the policy-makers haven't been able to decide on an allocation policy that limits the need to discard them.

A kidney transplant committee was formed by UNOS a decade ago to address this problem. For that decade, nothing has changed. The politics of rationing are to blame, where any reallocation creates life-changing winners and losers; youth versus age. A plan was finally proposed in 2011, similar to a successful policy established long ago in Europe, where discard rates are less than a third of those in the U.S. The plan called for rating each organ based on the donor's age, height, weight and medical history. The top 20 percent of those organs would be allocated to those candidates expected to live the longest. The rest would be matched to candidates within 15 years of the donor's age. However, the proposal died quickly after federal experts warned that discrimination laws would prohibit the use of age to determine outright who gets a transplant.

As a result, more kidneys that are suitable for transplant will be thrown away unnecessarily this year and every year that the transplant experts fail to establish an appropriate plan that will stem the problem - a plan that other countries have already successfully solved.

The transplant decision-makers, the experts, no matter how loudly they shout their opposition against changes in long-held policies, are not always right. With the continuing evolutions in technology, ethical views, social norms, the needs of society, and just plain common sense, the transplant community must continually reevaluate their rules to decide what is best for those who will die for lack of a needed organ or tissue. Yes, they have committees for precisely that purpose, but sometimes it seems that their rules were carried down Mt. Sinai with Moses himself, unchangeable because written by a divine finger. Several newspaper editorials over the years have claimed that the transplant policy-makers steadfastness is due to a penchant for political and bureaucratic control over medical decisions.

I'm not quite that cynical. To me, from my lowly place under the shoe of society, I believe that the policy-deciders sincerely want to find ways to save lives. I believe that many of them lose sleep over it regularly. But the shortage is such that any false move could make it worse. They must be cautious to a fault and slow to move for fear of negatively impact the very thing that we cannot afford to stigmatize.

However, when you've evaluated all the risk factors and you're left with obvious answers, or concerns that could potentially threaten public perception or reverse positive moves in donor numbers, it makes sense to pay attention to what makes sense to the very ones you are trying to encourage to become donors. To continue to discourage proposals that will increase the pool of donors for reasons that are long outdated and against what the majority, courts, those who need a donor and those who want to donate believe is common sense, you begin to negatively stigmatize yourselves. When you fail to make policies for fear of the potential political ramifications, even when you know it will work, you shame your field. When you are the deciding factor in who donates, when after decades of unyielding policies and over cautiousness you are the roadblock between the one who wants to donate and the life they could save, you are the one that is stigmatized. You cannot afford to be stigmatized, not when you have already failed so miserably at finding a lasting solution to the donor shortage. Not when so many lives continue to hang in the balance that are depending on you, the expert, to make the right policy-decisions that can save them.

An expert is a man who has made all the mistakes, which can be made, in a very narrow field... until he eventually knows the right way.

WOULDN'T HAVING A CRIMINALS ORGANS INSIDE ME BE DANGEROUS?

_____

_____

_____

FACTS:

37

THE NUMBER OF MOVIES, BOOKS AND OTHER MEDIA BASED ON MURDERERS ORGANS "LIVING ON" IN TRANSPLANT RECIPIENTS

0

THE TOTAL NUMBER OF DOCUMENTED OCCURRENCES OF PSYCHOPATHIC BEHAVIOR IN RECENT TRANSPLANT RECIPIENT ATTRIBUTED TO DONATED ORGANS.

CHAPTER 11

Can Prisoners' Traits 'Live On' in Donated Organs?

"DONATED CELLS REMAINED ENERGETICALLY AND NON-LOCALLY CONNECTED WITH THEIR DONOR."

-Paul Pearsall, Author 'The Hearts Code'

"Cellular memory" is a speculative belief that our personalities, tastes, habits, and histories are stored in human body cells independently of our genetic code or brain cells. The theory goes that if cells do in fact carry personality traits and preferences of individuals, then those traits can potentially be transferred through an organ transplant from donor to recipient. In other words, a recipient who preferred the color blue and fried chicken now finds himself adoring the color pink and eating only vegetarian meals.

Because our discussion is dealing with organ donations from inmates who conceivably include murderers and rapists, there is some concern that donations should not be allowed by such criminals just in case such a theory proves true. While it sounds like the work of creativity and fictional license, there is a segment of the science community who puts enough stock in this idea that it must be explored.

To most of us the story begins in Hollywood and the film industry who every decade or so churn out a script of horror themed by a transplanted body part which takes over the unsuspecting transplant recipient. This appeared at the infancy of films; all the way back to 1924 with Orlacs Hande a silent film adaptation of Les Mains d'Orlac (The Hands of Orlac) about a concert pianist who loses his hands in an accident. He receives a pair of freshly transplanted hands, which used to belong to a murderer. Of course, the respected pianist now develops the urge to kill.

Perhaps more notable was the 1991 film Body Parts adapted from the book Et Mon Tout est un Homme (authors of Vertigo) about a prison psychiatrist whose arm was severed in an accident. He is given the arm of an executed psychotic killer. Obviously, the arm has a mind of its own and it leads the formerly non-violent psychiatrist around on a killing spree.

Since we all know that Hollywood exaggerates for the sake of sensationalism and dramatic effect it's hoped that no one will wholeheartedly adopt the view that a killers transplanted body part will lead the rest of the recipients' body on a murderous rampage. However, what about the more subtle, ingrained traits and personality quirks, similar to the type we see inherited by children from their parents or sibling twins?

Most discussions of cellular memory begin with the experiences of Claire Sylvia, a recipient of a heart-lung transplant who wrote a book describing the changes she encountered post-transplant. Claire, a dancer and choreographer by trade, received her organs at Yale-New

Haven hospital on May 29, 1988 from an 18-year-old man who had been the victim of a motorcycle accident. On her way home from the hospital, she had an uncontrollable urge for KFC Chicken Nuggets, a food that her health-conscious former self would never before dream of eating. She then started noticing other changes in habits, tastes and overall attitudes. Thus began the makings of her 1997 book titled Change of Heart, later made into a 2002 Lifetime movie called <u>Heart of a Stranger</u> starring Jane Seymour.

It would be forgettable if Claire simply experienced preference changes such as her change in clothing from bright reds and oranges to cooler colors or her sudden cravings for green peppers and beer or chicken nuggets. Tastes change over time or due to dramatic adjustments in life circumstances, and no one would argue that an organ transplant is literally a life-altering moment in life. However, Claire also reported behaving in a more aggressive and impetuous manner that was uncharacteristic of her former self but which was supposedly distinctively similar to the personality of her donor. Her dancer demeanor was replaced with a more masculine presence. She no longer glided, she strutted.

In addition, she continually had dreams about a mystery man named Tim L., who she equally as mysteriously believed to be dreams of the prior owner of her heart. Upon meeting the "family of her heart", as she put it, Claire discovered that her donor's name was indeed Tim L. It was also revealed that her newly acquired attitudes, her cravings for green peppers and beer, her changes in preferences, the way she walked eerily resembled those of Tim. As it turned out, there were even uneaten KFC chicken nuggets that were found in her donors' jacket when he was killed.

With all of the makings of a Twilight Zone episode, Claire's experiences are difficult to ignore. Moreover, her encounters are not the only ones out there. In 2005, Nexus Magazine published a study administered by three PhD's on the subject.[120] As part of their article, they related ten individual case studies out of over seventy that were similar in nature to Claire's.

One of those was a 47-year-old white male with racist tendencies. Billy B.[121] received the heart of a young black male student who was the victim of a drive-by shooting. A troubling concern of the recipient was that his donor was black. Although he claimed that he wasn't racist, he stated derogatorily, "the idea of a black heart in a white body seems really...well, I don't know." His wife related that her husband actually asked her if he could ask the doctor for a white heart if one came up and he joked with his wife that he thought/ hoped his penis would grow to match the stereotypes of a black mans endowed features. He was quoted to have said, "I sometimes feel guilty because a black man made love to my wife."

Billy B. appeared somehow relieved to discover that after his transplant he had a newfound love of classical music. His wife stated, "He's driving me nuts with the classical music. He doesn't know the name of one song and never, never listened to it before. Now, he sits for hours and listens to it...You'd think he'd like rap music or something because of his black heart." His relief was that despite where his heart came from it didn't come packaged with any of the traits and preferences of what he assumed to be his donors.

What Billy B. didn't know at the time was that this 17-year-old black donor was killed on his way to violin class. He literally died hugging his violin case. He loved listening to classical music and playing along with it, despite the fact that the other kids made fun of him for it. Coincidence?

From a biased point of view, I want to emphasize that there is no actual scientific evidence to prove that cellular memory exists. Those favoring the strange and unproven fringe sectors of "science", such as mysticism, which set out to prove its existence, collected what "evidence" there is. Therefore, the case studies were published with some prejudice. One of the authors of the Nexus Magazine article, Paul Pearsall, a psychologist and author of The Pleasure Prescription and The Heart's Code, claims, "The heart has a coded subtle knowledge connecting us to everything and everyone around us. The aggregate knowledge is our spirit and soul...The heart is a sentient, thinking, feeling, communicating organ." He concludes, "Donated cells remained energetically and non-locally connected with their donor." Yet there was not a shred of scientific evidence to back his statements. These expressions remain unproven hypotheses.

Gary Schwartz, co-author of the Nexus article also believes that he understands the mechanism by which cellular memory works. "When the organ is placed in the recipient, the information and energy stored in the organ is passed on to the recipient. The theory applies to any organ that has cells that are interconnected. They could be kidneys, liver, and even muscles." Schwartz calls his belief a "theory", but it is not a theory in the sense that scientists use the term. His theory is based on the seeming fact that the "stories are compelling and consistent", stories which were collected in an attempt to prove that cellular memory exist. Cellular memory is, therefore, at best, an hypothesis.

It is risky business to collect stories for the sake of validating an hypothesis. Stories that seem to exhibit donor memories don't in themselves prove cellular memory. However, collecting a bunch of them could lead others to see a pattern that isn't really there. Until independent studies are done with all of the same safeguards, as scientifically reliable studies are required to have, I don't want to give this any undue credibility.

At least one professor tries to explain this phenomenon scientifically though. Dr. Candace Pert is a professor in the department of physiology and biophysics at Georgetown University and an expert in peptide pharmacology. She believes "the mind is not just in the brain but exists throughout the body." She claims, "The mind and body communicate with each other through chemicals known as peptides[122]." Peptides are found in the brain as well as in the stomach, muscles and all other major organs. Dr. Pert believes that memory can be accessed anywhere in the peptide/receptor network. "For instance, a memory associated with food may be linked to the pancreas or liver and such associations can be transplanted from one person to another." This sounds logical to my unscientific mind and such a theory would not cause any undue alarm in regards to inmate donations. However, Pert's notions have not found favor with neuroscientists who actually study the nature of memory. The evidence for her claims has yet to be produced.

I tend to lend more weight to other theories that have been advanced, again likely due to my bias. Some have theorized that recipients of a lifesaving organ so badly want to connect with their lifesaving donors that they may be subconsciously influenced by any tidbits of information that they pick up regarding their anatomical gifter. They discover what amounts to coincidence that turns into a connection, which is focused on so much that it is adopted as fact. It's referred to as "The Grapevine Theory", where pieces of personal information about the donor is overheard from staff conversations, perhaps even while the recipient is under anesthesia for their transplant itself or by other means, and these are subsequently adopted by the recipient as their own.

As for drastic changes in cravings and taste buds, I know from personal experience having been in a coma for a few days followed by pneumonia and other conditions that a drastic change in your health circumstances can at least temporarily affect your long ingrained desires. I have always drunk coffee as if it's required for my survival. I chain drink. I have done so since the age of 18. My Starbucks bill for a month at one time was breaching $300 on average. But this one major hospitalization had me so disgusted at the scent of it that my gag reflex would kick in, something that never happens for even the grossest of gross-outs. The thought of it repulsed me. I was suddenly off java for six months. I've come to my senses of course, but to me it was a dramatic change in my habits brought about by nothing more than a temporary change in my physiology or perhaps the unfamiliar medications in my system.

Some would describe this as "The Drug Theory" of cellular memory where an organ recipient may encounter similar experiences due to the required immunosuppressive drugs.

Dr. Jeff Punch, M.D. discusses the side effects of transplant medications such as Prednisone, which causes hunger and cellular memory. "The recipient of an organ transplant develops a love of pastry and finds out the person that donated their organ loved pastry as well. They think there is a connection, but really it is just the prednisone making their body crave sweets." Could it be as simple as that?

There is a part of me that pays attention to unexplained phenomenon though, perhaps similar to "The Quantum Theory" some have expressed. That theory posits that the answers may lie in a world that we are, as of yet, very ill equipped to prove, but such theorists take it a step further and try to explain it mathematically. Why do inanimate objects sometimes move? How can a man who can't tie his own shoes tell you 2,000 digits of pi while calculating the exact day of the week you were born on? How did the psychic know that my first dog was named "Rufus"?

I don't necessarily disbelieve that some can be especially "sensitive" to things that the average person is not. Nevertheless, even if this is the case, it is extremely rare at best and if someone were truly that receptive, I would think that they would already have a clue to their receptivity long before an organ transplant. If a particularly sensitive person had any concerns whatsoever over contracting traits from their donor, it seems likely that they would choose to decline an organ from someone who they fear may carry the negative traits of someone imprisoned. Although, I do believe that even if there is a segment of potential recipients who are really that sensitive, the traits carried over will never realistically meet the Hollywood bar of creating the homicidal psychopath out of a knitting grandma.

Some theories seem a little more out of left field in my opinion than others do. Nevertheless, for the sake of full disclosure I will relate them. Dr. Larry Dorsey believes a bit more cosmically that perhaps the most likely explanation "is that the consciousness of the donor had fundamentally united with the consciousness of the recipient enabling the recipient to gain information from the donor." A sort of Universal Mind theory.

James Van Praagh takes a more spiritual approach. He is quoted by Claire Sylvia as saying: "Donated organs often come from young people who were killed in car or motorcycle accident, and who quickly died. Because their spirits often feel they haven't completed their time on earth, they sometimes attach themselves to another person. There may be things that your donor hasn't completed in the physical world, which his spirit still wanted to experience."

There just isn't enough evidence out there now to say whether cellular memory is a realistic concern. Judging from the accounts and theories advanced, it can be argued that there is a need for further investigation. The relationship between the heart and the brain and the ways in which such a relationship affects one's physical, emotional, and mental health are being researched at various institutes. Perhaps one day we'll have a better understanding of this phenomenon.

In regards to organ donations by potentially dangerous offenders, there has never been a case related outside of fictional portrayals of anyone turning homicidal after having received a transplant from a dangerous donor. Critics will say that perhaps that's due to the fact that inmate donations are not widely accepted, hence the reason for this writing. However, even taking into account the studies from those who hypothesize that cellular memory is factual, these never overstepped the threshold of anything more than subtle traits, preferences, and personality quirks. Newly acquired appetites for violence or murderous transgressions are unrealistic concerns. If it is true that a donor can pass on such animalistic traits, then it might be unwise for people to obtain xenographic transplants from other species, such as baboons or pig valves, as do occur today.

However, due to the propensity of some to want to have a tight connection with their donor or those who are particularly sensitive in nature, it would be suggested that those certain personality types – discovered through the typical process of counseling that all organ recipients receive – should avoid inmate donations to prevent any undue psychological influence which could weigh on the minds of the recipient. Not only does that protect the recipient and those around them, but it prevents the development of any unwarranted stigma on inmate organ donations that Hollywood would be more than happy to perpetuate.

WOULD ALLOWING ORGAN DONATIONS FROM PRISONERS REALLY MAKE THAT MUCH OF A DIFFERENCE?

_____

_____

_____

FACTS:

8

THE AVERAGE NUMBER OF ORGANS THAT COULD POTENTIALLY BE DONATED BY ONE DECEASED PRISONER OR AFTER AN EXECUTION.

50+

THE ADDITIONAL TRANSPLANTABLE PARTS AND TISSUES THAT COULD BE DONATED BY ONE DECEASED PRISONER OR DEATH ROW INMATE.

8

THE POTENTIAL NUMBER OF LIVES LOST WITH EVERY EXECUTION OR DECEASED PRISONER THAT IS DENIED THE OPTION OF ORGAN DONATION.

COUNTLESS

THE NUMBER OF LIVES ALREADY LOST DUE TO THE EFFECTIVE BAN ON ORGAN DONATIONS FROM PRISONERS IN GENERAL.

PART FOUR

Progress Report

_____

_____

_____

CHAPTER 12

Recent Developments in Prisoner Organ Donation

The wish to donate healthy organs and tissue as a prisoner did not begin with me. Prisoners have been asking to donate since the relative infancy of organ transplantation in the country. Over time, other inmates, those in need of organs, legislators and even governors have attempted to find ways to make it so that any willing inmate could be considered for donation. Unfortunately, due to bumping against the wall that it the transplant community, not to even mention the formidable wall of the prison system, all of these efforts have fallen flat... until recently.

The reason for failure in most instances prior to now have to do with what was attached to the "donation". If there is one thing the transplant is industry is adamant about, beyond the health and safety of the transplants, is that organ donation in this country be done completely altruistically. If a donor is given anything for their anatomical gift, the gift is unacceptable. We saw it in their fight against the recent (and ongoing) litigation concerning the change in law allowing bone marrow donors to be compensated, and we've seen it the opposition to every proposal discussing donation from prisoners, death row or other wise.

For instance, in 1998, Missouri legislator Representative Chuck Graham proposed the "life-for-life" plan that would allow death row inmates to donate in exchange for a reduction of their sentence to life without parole.[123] To the transplant industry, this was tantamount to coercion and payment to an inmate for his "gift." The bill was squashed before it ever reached the Senate floor. Federal prison inmate, Clifford Bartz, outlined a bill that received some traction in scholarly journals to allow prisoners to donate their kidneys.[124] However, his effort was centered around a plan that would credit inmates with "good time" if they donated. Again, the transplant decision-makers panned the idea for offering incentives to donate.

As previously discussed, whether you agree or disagree with the transplant community's stance on compensation to the donor for offering a part of their body cannot be part of the discussion when it comes to donation from prisoners. As we've seen, the transplant community already has a chamber full of bullets they will fire at any prisoner donation proposal. Offering incentives are like handing them a rocket launcher. However, once you remove this coffin nail that is donor compensation, considerable progress can and has been made.

A Brief History of GAVE

As expressed at the outset, this mission began in 2009 as my wish to donate my healthy organs and tissue – any parts that could be re-used – both while I am alive and after I am executed. Upon learning this was "impossible", I began essentially making it my mission in life to make it possible. This won't redeem me for what I've done to get here, but I feel it's the best I can do from behind bars.

However, it became apparent early on that I needed support from outside the confines of my concrete cubicle if I was going to get anywhere in this effort. So with the help of anyone who could lend me a little time – my brother, an attorney who used to work on my death penalty appeals, a few others in my life who believed that this was a worthwhile effort – GAVE was established. From outward appearances, GAVE consists of a low budget website and a mediocre social media presence. However, this small presence has become a place for anyone interested in the topic of organ donation, especially for those questionably banned from participating, to go to for more information and to see how they could become involved in finding a solution. This has brought this issue from a 6x9 box to the entire world.

Behind the scenes, efforts include a continuous sending of letters to government agencies, politicians, the transplant community, hospitals, potential recipients, potential donors, corrections administrations, law schools, prison, gay rights and donations advocates, prison and gay rights groups, attorneys, and others. Responses have continued to include expert feedback, community & legal support, criminal justice and law school interest, and from many healthy but banned individuals who have seen value in the cause and who would like to be considered for organ donation.

Surveys and other projects have been initiated with various college schools legal, sociological, and criminal justice departments. It is necessary to continually evaluate the interest of prisoners, gay men and other groups in organ donation, the stated conflicts surrounding the reasons why no such donations have occurred until now, and to address the sociological concerns related to this topic. With academic input, G.A.V.E. hopes to gain support and validation within the scientific and transplant community – support that they feel is necessary if this is to be accepted on a meaningful level. They have established an informal registry for willing inmates – whether facing a death sentence or otherwise –- to make their wish known. GAVE provides information packets to all inmates who express interest in donating, which inform them of the hurdles surrounding inmate donation and organ donation in general, as well as what they can do within their prisons to best make their wish of organ donation a reality. For those inmates facing execution, GAVE tracks the status of those inmates who have reached the end of their appeals and who are facing imminent executions. When an execution date has been set, a packet goes out to that inmate expressing the option of organ donation and suggestions on how to approach the prisons administration and local government to consider the option should they determine that it is something that they want to pursue. GAVE encourages the inmate to respond with any questions or for any assistance they might need in taking up the issue with their prison as well as offering additional resources through its websites for family and friends of those condemned.

Early on, however, it became apparent that it wasn't going to be enough to stay behind the scenes. I've always been conflicted between staying off the radar, for the sakes of those who I have hurt terribly with my past actions, and trying to bring about some measure of decency from my circumstances. It was quickly becoming obvious, though, that this effort would fan out without a more concerted vocal push. We weren't really sparking the debate necessary to turn this into the flame it needed to be to forge change. Therefore, we began advocacy efforts directly through the media and other publications to try to fan that embers.

The first published article appeared on the cover of the November 2010 issue of Compassion, a bi-monthly publication designed to encourage death row inmates to do something positive with their remaining time. The publication reached all of the 3300 death row inmates in the U.S. -- the only publication to do so. This allowed GAVE the platform to reach the audience most affected by the idea of organ donations after execution without having to physically mail thousands of letters and while avoiding the unnecessary sensationalism of traditional media.

Realizing the power of traditional media, however, GAVE has consistently courted some in the press who could potentially be of assistance in raising awareness. Unflattering articles have appeared in publications nationwide regarding me, including books, magazine print media such as Vanity Fair and Esquire, as well as local press. While these have not concentrated solely on my organ donation intentions and have quite possibly served to undermine my efforts on some level, it has opened doors that have serve ultimately to bring about some of the desired results. For instance, it allowed the opportunity of being published in the March 6th, 2011 issue of the Sunday New York Times[125], a prominent place that irritated many, but that had the desired effect of getting the debate going. It was the top-talked about opinion piece that day as well as number eight on the NYT's Top Ten Stories list. It not only fanned the flame, it caused a forest fire around the globe. This opened the door for the cause to be seen on every major television news network in over 20 countries, over 150,000 separate webpage's, over 1,100 separate blog sites, and sparked interest from seven different documentary film companies ranging from the hour-long variety you see on the Discovery Channel and MSNBC, to HBO and big screen productions, solely on the issue of organ donation from prisoners. GAVE continues to field inquiries for articles, books, and TV and movie productions from various national and international media outlets.

Better than all of that, but likely because of it, this has allowed the possibilities of prisoner organ to be seen by those who can actually do something to make this a reality... which it has started to become.

Progress

Prisoners all along have asked to be able to donate their healthy parts. In the last few years, however, these requests have been far more frequent and loud. Hundreds of prisoners have approached GAVE annually to ask how they can convince their prison system to allow them to donate. Through education of the roadblocks to provide a better understanding as to why their prison decision-makers have repeatedly denied them this option, and with suggestions on better avenues, as well as much support as could be provided from my cubicle, prisoners have begun to be more vocal in their requests and are now making inroads. With a little knowledge, thousands have registered as organ donors.

In 2012, after finding out about a dying inmate who was refused the ability to donate his organs, U.S. Representative Steve Eliason, of Utah, proposed legislation for prisoner organ donation that did not include incentives for the donor. His proposed law was simple: Allow inmates to be register and be considered for organ donation, just as any other U.S. citizen can. After passing unanimously through both the House and the Senate, Governor Gary R. Herbert signed the first prisoner organ donation bill into law in March of 2013. Utah became the first state to legislate an inmate's right to be an organ donor – a state that is arguably the most conservative in these United States.

Now, upon check-in to a Utah state penitentiary, you are asked – just as you would be at the DMV – if you would like to register as an organ donor. Within six months of the laws signing, fifteen percent of all prison inmates in Utah are now registered organ donors.

The unanimous – who I'll continue to highlight as something special -- passing through legislative chambers has prompted other state legislators to look at the issue. As of this writing, Oklahoma is finishing the final draft of its prison organ donation bill, while Wisconsin is beginning theirs. GAVE is continuing to work hard to get other states to do the same.

More recently, there has been a major change of wind in the fight to allow organ donation from executed inmates in at least one state. In November 2013, Governor John Kasich of Ohio granted a temporary stay of execution to Ohio death row inmate Ronald Phillips. Phillips had requested that his organs be donated promptly after execution. His mother was on dialysis and needed a kidney, and his sister was in need of a heart due to a chronic heart condition. Even if he wasn't a match for either of them, however, he asked that his organs be gifted to anyone else in need.

The prison quickly rejected the donation request, citing safety and security concerns. Also, according to the prison spokesperson, "The department is not equipped to facilitate organ donation pre- or post-execution." The day before the execution, though, Governor Kasich stepped in to give the matter a more thorough consideration, buying the prison eight more months to figure it out. As he stated, "This is a bit of uncharted territory. But if another life can be saved by his willingness to donate his organs and tissues, then we should allow for that to happen." The Governor is still getting a standing ovation from GAVE. Phillips is now scheduled for execution in July 2014. He may become the first death row inmate to ever be allowed to donate after an execution, finally setting the long overdue precedent that may end up saving hundreds of lives.

In addition, several states prisons and county jails have begun enacting organ donation policies on their own. One notable effort has come from the controversial Sheriff Arpaio out of Maricopa County, Arizona. In 2007, he started the "Inmates Donating Organs (I DO) program in his county's jail system, educating inmates of the need for organs in the U.S. through a video and poster campaign, and asking them if they would like to be a part of the solution and register as organ donors. There is no incentive offered to do so, only a postcard that is sent out to each registered inmates family informing them of the inmates' registration on Arizona's donor list.

The Sheriff's department had a stated goal of signing up 10,000 inmates. As of the date of this writing, almost 15,000 inmates have signed up voluntarily in that one county alone.

The Federal Bureau of Prisons (FBP) and a few state prison systems -- Texas, Ohio, Utah, Georgia and Arizona - have added procedures that allow some inmates to donate. However, these are fairly limiting in scope. For instance, most will only allow prisoners to donate when the recipient is blood-related, such as to a sibling, parent or biological child. While the FBP does specify that donations to non-relatives may be considered on a "case-by-case" basis, there is no record of them ever allowing a living donation from an inmate to a stranger, or generally after death.

While the prison policies that are beginning to be written are not perfect in their ability to save the lives of those on the organ waiting lists today, it's a start. A few years ago, there were no prisoner organ or tissue donation policies at all. Now there are prisons registering inmates as they walk in the fortified door. Legislators are stepping up to ensure that inmates are given the option of donation. Governors are stepping in to make sure that prisons carefully consider the options before instantly rejecting an inmates request to donate. But for every prison director, legislator, or governor who is beginning to take a closer look, there are dozens who are ignoring the issue.

As we've discussed, the transplant community moves at a glacial pace. The prison systems move almost as slowly. That is why it is so vital to keep pressing on, helping to educate the policy-makers of the possibilities and realities of prisoner organ donation today. There is no continuing legitimate reason to prevent inmates from donating healthy parts right now. Literally, the longer it takes to establish policies and procedures to ease the road to organ donation from inmates, the more people die unnecessarily.

In the meantime, we'll help facilitate prisoners to shout from the rooftops, to their prison directors, state legislators, governors, to local media, through anyone who can make the necessary positive change. Perhaps it'll come through the continuing campaigns, or documentaries, or any other effort we can think of to try. On the other hand, maybe it'll come from a wake-up call, when somebody who has the power to influence policy comes face-to-face with a loved one who cannot get a needed organ or tissue in time to save them because there just aren't enough to go around. As painful as that is to consider, that is the reality for the majority of those who has a loved one on a waiting list right now. A pointless reality.

CHAPTER 13

What Can You Do?

"(IN) A DEMOCRATIC SOCIETY LEGISLATURES, NOT COURTS, ARE CONSTITUTED TO RESPOND TO THE WILL AND CONSEQUENTLY THE MORAL VALUES OF THE PEOPLE."

Chief Justice Warren Burger
U.S. Supreme Court
Gregg v. Georgia, 96 S. Ct. at 2926

What can you do?

That depends. Who are you? Are you every day Joe Citizen? Are you someone who needs an organ or tissue? Are you someone who spends your days around criminals either as a prison administrator, corrections officer, or a criminal yourself? Are you someone who gets to help set guidelines or make law, either as a legislator or as a transplant policy-maker? Do you know someone who is? Whoever you are, there's something that you can do to help advance the rights of prisoners to donate organs and tissue.

Most of Us

Obviously, being the author of this publication, and an obnoxious advocate yelling to try to make prisoner organ and tissue donation a reality, the fact that you're reading this line and the thousands of lines that got you to this point is a great start, in my opinion. When I first began this mission, I didn't really know where to begin either. I figured that I could slap together a website – which in itself turned out to be a pretty daunting undertaking from a prison cell – and people would flock to the idea, rolling into enough support to jumpstart it without much more active participation needed on my part. I already knew that there were enough prisoners who wanted to donate. There was certainly more than a sufficient amount of people who believed that prisoners should have the right to donate. My hope was that few of those would be transplant professionals, or prison directors, or maybe a governor or two, and that this would eventually open up as an accepted practice.

If that failed, I decided that I would take the issue to court, and let them tell the world that prisoners have as much of a right to be organ and tissue donors as every other healthy person in this country. I was already aware that it wasn't illegal for prisoners to donate. There was no statute that prohibited anatomical gifts from inmates. I would just need a court to explain to the powers that be that this translated into a right that I had. Prison is a sue-happy place, and for a minute, I fell into the thought that this would be the way to resolve this dilemma.

However, then I came across the above quote from a former Chief Justice of our great lands highest court, and it got me readjusting my thoughts on the subject.

We have already established that every excuse used to state why prisoner organ donation cannot occur is outdated and invalidated. The majority of those in the U.S., prisoner and free man alike, are supportive of prisoner donation – many, in fact, thought that it was already taking place. The only real concern that remains is one that is more subjective, ethical issues that cannot simply be determined by somebody, or even a group of people agreeing that it should be one way or another.

When it comes to an issue like this that the public is for, that obviously saves lives, and that all parties involved can see benefit from, but that is prevented by a handful of people because it is ethically concerning, there has to be a way to express the will and support of the people as a whole. Fortunately, we have a process for that. The legislative process. If it's not against the law, but it sits in a spot that doesn't explicitly grant the right to force the issue, we need some clarification in the form of state statutes. There just happen to be hundreds of legislators around the U.S. who have the power to sponsor such movements, who are more than happy to take up a logical position that already has widespread support and little opposition.

"Write your congressman" is an annoying phrase that doesn't exactly elicit a gung-ho spirit. Most people don't have the time in their day to write out their grocery list, much less a thought-out letter to a professional who is probably far too busy to read a letter from the little people in their midst. It's hard to fathom that our wish will be given much attention, much less carried out by a busy senator or representative of our state. But, it works.

Utah became the first proof of that in 2013. By being made aware if inmate wishes to donate organs and to find a legislative way to help make that become a reality through simple letters, a U.S. Representative in the Utah legislature decided to sponsor a prisoner organ donation bill. The process took the bill to Utah's House of Representatives and then to the state Senate floor. It should be noted that Utah is one of the, if not THE most conservative state of our union. It is not typically an easy thing to pass legislation of any kind through their legislature. However, the bill not only passed with a majority, it passed through both chambers unanimously!

Within a few short months, the Governor of Utah had it on his desk and signed it into law. Utah became the first state to successfully legislate the right for prisoners to be organ and tissue donors. Now the Utah prison system actually asks each inmate as they enter the prison system there if they would like to be organ or tissue donors, just like the rest of the U.S. public is asked by the DMV when they renew their licenses. There are now over 1,000 of the 7,000 prisoners in Utah registered as organ donors.

One down, 49 to go.

Again, it sounds a little daunting, but due the *unanimous* passing in one state, several other state legislators are taking notice. But they're not doing so on their own. They are taking notice because they are being sent letters and emails by those who want prisoner organ donation to be a reality. If you're reading this chapter because you want to know what you can do to advance this effort, write you congressman. I'll even make it easy for you. In the appendix is a sample letter that you can copy and paste to an email as your own, or print it out and send it to your local congressional representative of choice. If you're not sure who that is, simply click on: http://www.vote-smart.org   It's a quick and easy search by zip code.

Still not your cup of tea? Join our online community. Through our website, facebook and twitter pages, blogs, and other social network options, the topic is discussed freely, and there are often calls for specific needs through those sites that you may find more up your alley. I would encourage you to sign on and be an active participant. Some of the sites of note are linked at the end of this chapter.

If you're more the type who prefers to donate to an effort worth contributing to, everything from the sale of this book to donations sent through links on the recommended sites go directly to further this cause. Your support can go a long way towards furthering this effort, thanks to many volunteers who have more time than resources.

Legislators

Obviously, from the quote at the outset of this chapter, I regard legislators with the highest esteem because I believe that you are in a position to help the most. Thanks to a few courageous forward-thinking U.S. Representatives and state Senators, this issue is already seeing the light of day in a few legislative chambers. A few is certainly a good start, but we need more if prisoners are truly going to be able to positively influence the donor pool.

As mentioned above, the legislators who have already tackled this topic, raising it as a proposed bill on their House or Senate floors, have been able to not only do so successfully, but triumphantly. Unanimous support through both House and Senate is nothing to balk at or take lightly. Properly worded, a bill to create law legislating an inmate's right to be a donor can easily be passed. The reason for this is likely that it's time has come and it just makes sense. There's no better to imitate that success than to emulate the process where success was found. Therefore, in the appendix of this book, I have provided you with all of the information you will need to put together a bill that you can sponsor and carry to successful law creation. I have provided the contact information of previous successfully sponsored bills, as well as text from the actual laws that were proposed and adopted. Additionally, other sponsored legislation will be updated and available on the GAVE website. (http://www.gavelife.org)

Thank you, in advance, for your consideration of this topic. Your sponsorship can literally save lives. I can't imagine a greater change in law than that.

Prison Dwellers

Whether you live in a prison or work at one, there are ways that you can help advance this cause from within. Besides contacting and gaining support from the area legislators, as mentioned previously, you have the power to actually affect rule change from behind the walls.

Every prison system in the U.S. has a method for proposing rule changes within the prison. By law, the prison must tell you how to suggest or propose these rule changes in a way that they will be seriously considered by the powers-that-be in your prison system. Typically, due to the frequent need of prison systems to adjust with the times, whether the "times" come in the form of changes in state law or at the hands of creative prisoners who figured out ways to bend the rules beyond their intended tensile strength, there are something akin to "Rule Coordinators" whose sole job is to maintain the prisons rules as they change or are proposed. These coordinators make sure that the suggested rule/policy changes comport with the state-mandated ways of making administrative policy changes, to ensure that law is not violated in the process of these changes. While most of the rule-changes that are requested are proposed by the prison system itself, the methods for proposing rule-changes can be made by anyone, whether you're a prisoner, prison guard, or a concerned citizen.

Propose a rule change. If your prison system does not already have a published organ or tissue donation policy, propose one. You'll need to contact your prison administrators to determine what the appropriate method is for doing so in your prison system. But once you've gotten to that point, the rest is simple. In the appendix, I've provided a sample proposed rule that will make it possible for prisoners in your state to be able to be considered for organ and tissue donation. Additionally, information will be provided and updated through the GAVE website, and assistance can be given through any of the GAVE contacts. Visit the site, make contact with GAVE, or have friends or family help you to make contact.

However you decide to help, you are contributing to the saving of innocent lives, lives that will be lost if prisoner organ and tissue donation is not more widely accepted. Thank you in advance for your support.

To support GAVE's efforts, please visit:

http://www.gavelife.org

http://facebook.com/G.A.V.E.PrisonerOrganDonation

http://www.twitter.com/G.A.V.E_Life

christianlongo@gavelife.org

Direct mail contact:

Christian Longo #14509855
Oregon State Penitentiary
2605 State Street
Salem, Oregon 97310

Remember, you can save a life today. Register to be a donor now:

Organ Donor Registry: http://www.unos.org

Bone Marrow Registry: http://www.BeTheMatch.org

Scientific Registry: http://www.UStransplant.org

CONCLUSION

We have addressed what have become the main arguments against prisoner organ and tissue donations. At best, these are cautionary tales emphasizing what we need to be aware of when developing the necessary safeguards to implement organ donation policies that include prisoners. At worst, these are nothing more than excuses to introduce fear and to discourage the public from such policies due to fears of the controversial. As we've seen, though, the public and even many experts cannot deny the plausibility and the obvious benefits of allowing such donations to take place from willing prisoners.

Since these major arguments are satisfied through reasonable discussion and research, all that's left is subterfuge, introduced as a further attempt to deter the adoption of these policies. Some say, in the case of the executed, that there aren't enough potential donors to make a difference, "so why are we even talking about it?" Only about 50 executions take place each year. However, if just half of those donated – a number far below recent death row survey findings of those who would be willing to do so – over 200 lives could be saved each year. To look at it another way, there have been about 5000 innocent lives that have perished needlessly over the last couple of decades from blocking death row donations. That is not an insignificant number – and that's not counting all of the other prisoners who want to donate. Regardless, it's not the quantitative affect that is most important. It's the fact that somebody survived because of a healthy, quality organ donated by someone who was willing and able to give it. Look at your partner or child or friend and say that's not worth it.

Other arguments that have been expressed are shot-in-the-dark speculations. For instance, some argue that allowing prisoners to donate will stigmatize non-prisoner donations. It will present a "Why should I donate if a prisoner can 'pay back society' by donating" argument, and other donations will shrink as a result. The simple counter to that is that those who are altruistic enough to part with an organ would likely not think in those terms. Also, we have other comparisons to disprove such a theory. Prisoners frequently assist in times of natural disasters due to the great need for willing extra hands. Inmates fight forest fires, help during oil spills along the Gulf of Mexico, and assist in flood-ravaged regions such as during the aftermath of hurricane Katrina in Louisiana. Public participation is not deterred in those areas and it's likely that organ donations from those who want to help would be similarly unaffected. The reality though is that nobody - from the experts on down - knows what sort of impact these newly adopted policies would have. The only certainty is that lives are being lost by the reluctance to even consider it

So what's the real problem?

As I stated in the introduction, I don't presume to know all that a transplant professional or prison administration knows or must consider when weighing the issues surrounding prisoner organ donations. I only know what objections they voice to it and the roadblocks they raise to tell me that it can't be done. Then I dig to find the facts of the matter myself.

A few things are apparent after having dug through those tens of thousands of pages of reports and history. If the transplant community ever came knocking on the prison gates to discuss the possibility of promoting organ donations behind its walls, the prison would scoff in an 'absolutely not' fashion. They are still too sore from the discovered abuses from decades ago, and the lawsuits that followed, to even consider such a medically unnecessary idea.

If the prison directors ever came knocking on the office doors of the transplant community proposing to organize a way for prisoners to more easily donate organs while living, or after execution, the transplant community wouldn't answer. The high-profile nature of another countries transplant abuses alone are enough to make them forever squeamish.

In many cases, it doesn't matter to either what the facts are, as shown in this book. It's a reflex reaction by some brought about by perceptions that should no longer be valid. It's as if some in the transplant community is more concerned about the potential for urban legends that might form through adoption of these policies than they are about evolving with the times. This policy is one that could actually provide a solution to a shortage problem that the transplant community have thus far been stumped as to how to fix. However, it's essentially a can of worms that they just don't want to open.

Many prison systems simply don't change unless they are forced to through some government adjustment or through litigation – especially if it touches on an issue they have been sued for in the past and lost, no matter how far in the past it was. It doesn't matter that it's potentially a tremendous positive for the community they serve. It's something they aren't required to do, so they won't without a huge shove in that direction.

The main push, though, is coming from a death row inmate, someone who is screaming from the dungeon of society. Someone who some say has been stripped of the privilege to have a voice. Because I took life, I cannot be human enough to care about the organ shortage or to have a logical point. Even if it is believable that I care about someone enough to want to fight for their life and others in their position, it must be a convenient ploy to stand on a stage distracting away from the horrible things that I did to land here. If it's not that, maybe it's so that I can get a shot at redemption for having done so much wrong, as the noted ethicist stated I shouldn't have the privilege of.

The facts are that I don't feel as though I can or should be redeemed. In that sense, I agree with that ethicist. I was torn for years about raising my voice for this issue. I didn't want the attention because it distracted from the lives I took. It would stir up the pains of those I hurt. I tried to simply ensure that I could at least give my healthy organs away by quietly approaching my prison administration, offer to cancel my remaining appeals and face the sentence that I was rightly given. However, the prison denied me.

That the prison could deny such a request, and without any reason, was ridiculous to me. They'd rather let eight or more people die for lack of my healthy organs? For what? Inconvenience? Potential ethical concerns? Maybe for the simple reason that it was me asking something that I wanted to do? It would turn out later that that was it. Their official statement to the press: "We do not have interest as a department in negotiating with Mr. Longo."[126]

I considered shouting from that first denial, but I knew what it would entail. I knew what the perception would be. I knew that it would perpetuate the hurt I had caused. I know that those I hurt would rather that I rot quietly in my dungeon. I see it every time in the comments section wherever news comes out with my name attached to it, or frequently on GAVE's Facebook wall. I understand it. I would do the same thing, if not more, if the tables were turned. Maybe I've lost the privilege of being able to do something positive from my circumstances. Maybe I squandered my chance. I am sincerely sorry that those I hurt have to know that I am still breathing, much less talking loudly enough for others to hear me. They should have the voice, not me.

To look at it from another seat, though, if I did not stand up from the pit I deserve to be in, you would not be giving this topic of life-saving potential any serious consideration, at least until another me came along with the same drive and passion from this topic. In the meantime, a bunch of other people who didn't deserve it would also be dead. Preventing me from arguing this is not worth the hundreds, maybe even thousands, who could potentially be saved, or the 8 more lives my body alone could save, or the life of the best friend who motivated this effort, and whose life should have the chance of enhancing the lives of many who are far more deserving than me.

The compromise has become GAVE It was established with the idea of building a movement to fight for those who are going to die without willing prisoners donated organs. It's my hope that it continues to grow enough to let me go back to where I belong – below the sightline of those I've hurt, preferably deeply enough that my organs can be of benefit to those who need them more than I do. I intend to fight out front for as long as my voice is needed, but not a second more. So if you hate the sound of my voice, support GAVE.

With support, GAVE will expand its research and education efforts to prove to the prison and the transplant communities that prisoner organ donation – as well as donation from other similarly unnecessarily banned groups, like gay men and hemophiliacs – makes sense and are possible now. We will continue our work with legislators and universities to create law, gauge prisoner interest, the publics' approval, and any conflicts that must be considered. It is our hope that GAVE's data, arguments, and support will be overwhelmingly convincing as to not be ignored by the gatekeepers.

There are over 135,000 people in the U.S. on waiting lists dying for a lack of a healthy donor organ or tissue. Twenty-four of them will die today. It doesn't have to be this way.

There is understandable fear of the controversial. However, concerns from decades past and speculation over what permitting organ donations from prisoners might result in overlooks the fact that many lives are being lost right now. With nearly 2 million prisoners and over 3000 on death row, the potential to save some of those lives is dramatic.

Shari[127], from the prologue, exists, and many like her. For her, or anyone who would be able to have a longer, more fulfilling and satisfying life with a healthy organ or tissue donation, to continue to suffer until they eventually die is a tragedy. Knowing that they could have gotten the organ or tissue they needed from a willing donor who was denied simply because they were incarcerated is even worse than a tragedy, because it was unnecessary. Please support prisoner organ and tissue donation before another Shari dies needlessly.

Christian M. Longo

christianlongo@gavelife.org

ACKNOWLEDGEMENTS

The organization of GAVE and all that it entails could not happen without a great amount of passion and trust in what GAVE is trying to accomplish. Foremost, I thank Shawna Wilson for being my motivation to start this mission and to keep it moving forward despite the hurdles, for being my best friend, and for continuing to share this passion with me. Your shoulders are small, but you have carried the great weight of all that life has thrown at you, and all that comes with having me in your life. Without your strength, sacrifices, forgiveness, and your families willingness to share you with me, GAVE would only be a hope.

Life in a box – even with the passion of one other – does not exactly lend to a successful endeavor. I am therefore constantly appreciative to of all who have provided support. To my brother Dusty, for tech support and for continuing to be my brother despite it all. To my legal support – especially Harry – for allowing me to the use of their expertise, resources, and other assistance, even when it contradicted with their fight for my life. To the unwavering support from Erik and the continuing assistance and encouragement from Joe, Brian, Dewayne, Elaine, Shannon, Jeffrey, James, and even Mike. You've not only made this publication possible, but you've also helped push GAVE ahead through intense opposition from the "experts" by sticking with me when I needed more troops. To my good friend Dave, who continually let me bore him with my nonstop rants about organ donation. And to the expertise and support of Dr. K, who proved that even some of the "experts" are on the side of this mission.

Nothing that I can do will ever cure the pain that I have caused or bring back the lives that I have destroyed. This effort, my organs, or GAVE cannot redeem me in any way. However, those who have found value in this mission and who continue to support it are participating in the saving of many innocent lives that would otherwise be lost without them. Thank you to all who recognize this and who offer their assistance and encouragement despite me.

Christian M. Longo --christianlongo@gavelife.org

ABOUT THE AUTHOR

Christian Longo was incarcerated on Oregon's death row in 2003 at the age of 30. He pleaded guilty to the murders of his wife and youngest daughter, and was found guilty for the murders of his eldest daughter and son. After the mandatory review and affirming of his case by the Oregon Supreme Court, and upon consideration of his circumstances, his guilt, and the medical issues of the one who became his motivation to donate his organs, he decided to forego his remaining appeals and face his sentence. Before his execution, he petitioned the Oregon State Penitentiary to allow him to donate a kidney to the friend in need and his remaining organs and tissues to anyone else on transplant waiting lists. However, the Oregon prison system denied his request, essentially rejecting it on the basis that there were too many challenges to allowing organ donation from prisoners to non-family members – especially from death row.

In 2009, after extensively researching the complications of organ donations from prisoners, and learning that these concerns were severely outdated and unnecessary, Longo established Gifts of Anatomical Value from Everyone (GAVE). The objective of GAVE is to educate prisons, the transplant community and the public of the modern realities of prisoner organ donation. It is their mission to convince the transplant policy-makers that it is now safe and makes sense to begin accepting the organs and tissues of healthy willing prisoner donors. With over 2 million inmates in the U.S., prisoners could make a tremendous impact on the organ shortage in this country. GAVE intends to prove that this is possible now.

Longo has been published by the New York Times and in numerous smaller publications. His mission has garnered the interest of hundreds of news outlets and thousands of websites around the globe. The attention brought to prisoner organ donation through Longo and GAVE has prompted many prisoners to step forward to announce their wish to donate and has also influenced several legislators to consider the option of establishing law that mandates an inmates right to be an organ and tissue donor. In 2013, after unanimously passing through both House and Senate, Utah became the first state to successfully add a prisoner organ donation statute. As of this writing, Oklahoma, Wisconsin, and Texas, along with other state legislators are drafting similar prisoner organ and tissue donation bills for their legislatures to likewise consider.

It is hoped that through this publication, the continuing education through GAVE, the evolution of the transplant community to catch up with current advancements, and the bravery of policy-makers and legislators, healthy prisoner organ and tissue donation will become a common reality which soon saves uncountable lives.

To support GAVE's efforts, please visit:

http://www.gavelife.org

http://facebook.com/G.A.V.E.PrisonerOrganDonation

http://www.twitter.com/G.A.V.E_Life

christianlongo@gavelife.org

Write directly to:

Christian Longo
2605 State Street
Salem, Oregon 97310

Remember, you can save a life today. Register to be a donor now:

Organ Donor Registry: http://www.unos.org

Bone Marrow Registry: http://www.BeTheMatch.org

Scientific Registry: http://www.UStransplant.org

APPENDIX

SUMMARY OF CONFLICTS

- ORGAN DONATIONS FROM THE CONDEMNED

- ORGAN DONATIONS FROM WILLING INMATES

LETTER TO STATE LEGISLATORS

INFO FOR STATE LEGISLATORS

- SAMPLE BILL

- CONTACT INFO FOR SUCCESSFUL SPONSORS

PROPOSED PRISON POLICY CHANGE

GAVE MISSION STATEMENT

Summary of Conflicts

Organ Donations From the Condemned

Why organ donation from the executed is not occurring now:

- Lethal Injection has not allowed for viable organ donations until now.

- Much opposition has come from the medical community, the transplantation industry, & anti-death penalty groups, primarily due to perceived ethical considerations.

- China's practices have discouraged use of organs from the condemned out of fears of stigmatization.

Lethal Injection Protocols

(See 'Chapter 7: Doesn't Lethal Injection Kill the Organs?')

<u>The typical 3-drug protocol has disallowed viable organ donations.</u>

- Now a 1-drug protocol is available using a single barbiturate..

- Ohio, South Dakota & Washington have adopted this new protocol.

- This 1-drug protocol allows for viable organ donations, according to expert Dr. David Waisel, Harvard Associate Professor of Anesthesiology, and others

Medical Community Concerns

(See 'Chapter 8: Will Physicians Participate?')

<u>Participation in procuring organs from the condemned violates Hippocratic Oath.</u>

- Arguments against abortion & assisted-suicide relied on this same Oath.

- Oath comprised of 10 points, 7 of which are violated on a significant scale[128], such as 'an abortive remedy'.

- Doctors readily adapt to changing legal climate once considered ethical by the general public and courts.

<u>AMA prohibits physician participation.</u>

- 41% of physicians polled would violate AMA prohibition against assisting in capital punishment.(2001 poll of 413 physicians') [129]

- AMA contradicts itself repeatedly. AMA opposed women becoming doctors, health insurance, abortions, birth control, assisted suicide, Medicare, etc.

- Less than 1 in 3 doctors are AMA members.

- AMA actually makes organ donation permissible in its capital punishment guidelines. (AMA Opinion 2.06).

Physicians do not want to be seen as executioners.

- Non-medical staff administers lethal injection. Physicians call death, ensure dead donor is transferred quickly for donation & procures organs.

- Similar to doctors open actions in Death with Dignity / assisted suicide.

- Doctors who oppose do not have to participate.

Transplant Industry Opposition

(See 'Chapter 3: Prisoners Are Disgusting & Chapter 4 Testing Prisoners for Infectious Disease')

Prison is a high-risk environment for infectious diseases and transmission.

- Technological advancement in testing such as RNA testing has drastically improved in recent years.[130]

- False positives are more likely than the feared false negatives.

- Timeframe for testing better than for any accident victim, as is currently the primary method for obtaining organs

Racial & Economic Class Imbalance

- Concerns are based on prejudiced testing on African Americans from the 1930's to 70's. (Tuskegee Syphilis Trials)

- History shows minorities are less likely to participate in inmate medical options However, such a program could theoretically be a boost to the number of minority donations

- Proper public awareness regarding the methods of consent and the purely voluntary nature could counter adverse debate.

- Nobody really knows what sort of impact this will have on minority donations. So far, it's conjecture.

Stigma: Public Will be Less Inclined to Donate/ Will Get Negative Publicity

- Prior negative publicity (in the 80's) had an entirely different landscape of donor difficulties. (Less than 30k on waiting lists then compared with over 112k today.)

- Proposal already has wide public support. [131]

- Other inmate-assisted programs (i.e. forest fire fighting, natural disaster support) do not deter public participation by public

Not Enough Potential Donors to Make a Difference.

- One execution can save from 6-12 lives.

- Program would save more lives than recently publicized programs instituted by procurement organizations.[132]

- 50% of condemned inmates would donate upon execution, per studies done through California University. Long Beach.[133]

- See 'China Syndrome' below.

- Since the mid-80's there have been over 1100 executions and anywhere from 3,000 – 6,000 missed life-saving opportunities. Over 100 lives could be saved annually. (Potentially 300+)

- Even if it is proven that there are too few death row donors to have a large impact, it the quality of the act, not the quantitative effects from a situation that otherwise bears nothing positive.

Anti-Death Penalty Opposition

Anything that brings a positive to the death penalty could increase its use.

- Lethal injection is already considered humane by the Supreme Court [134]and the public in general

- Certain states will not likely move away from capital punishment anytime soon. If the punishment must remain then it should be implemented in a way that brings about something positive for all involved.

- Focus should shift to those who must die but who have no opportunity to do so in a dignified & positive way.

General Capital Punishment Concerns

Publicity surrounding organ donation would overshadow the crime & victim.

- Arguments made for this in the past5 had to do with negative publicity towards the punishment itself. [135]

- Organ donation can be achieved anonymously.

- The only reasons to publicize donations are to raise awareness prior to any decision to allow donation from condemned inmates.

- If publicity were necessary, it can be done in a way that emphasizes the benefits to the community and with support from the victims themselves.

- Get victims input through prisons victims' programs.

China Syndrome

(See: Chapter 6: China's Bad Example)

<u>Since China has become known as a country that frequently abuses death row inmates by harvesting their organs, some ethicists express concern that by allowing such donations in the U.S. altruistic donations here would be stigmatized and potentially shrink other donation figures.</u>

- China's practices related to the death penalty cannot be compared with the U.S.

- China executes 15,000/year. 69% are for non-violent offenses such as drug dealing & open practice of religion. Many convicted after rushed trials based on confessions extracted under torture.[136]

- To use the same argument, due to China's abhorrent death penalty practices the U.S. should not have the death penalty either. Nevertheless, it does.

- The issue is not insurmountable with open communication with experts in the field

- The U.S. has an organization of safeguards and guidelines to ensure consent for organ donation[137]. These same guidelines, plus other constructed specifically for willing death row inmates, would be used in such donations.

- The U.S already has shown wide support for such donations. (See 'Stigma" under Transplant Industry)

Ethical Dilemmas

(See Chapter 9: Is Prisoner Organ Donation Ethical?)

Death row inmates are there to be punished and should not be allowed to do anything that detracts from that punishment. It clouds the issue of capital punishment and glorifies a condemned inmate.

- Some well known ethicists believe that if death row prisoners could do something obviously positive from their circumstances it would give that condemned man an unworthy redemption before dying..

- The very temporary satisfaction a condemned man may get would be short-lived, as he would be executed thereafter. However, it gives several innocent people the more permanent satisfaction of life through their newly received organs, which easily balances any ethical conflict.

Logistical Considerations

With no hospital on the premises and considering the organ donation communities apprehensions in regards to donations from condemned inmates, there may be numerous logistical complications.

Transplantation Facilities

- Since execution must take place at the prison, [138] it is necessary to provide makeshift facilities for the procurement of organs. This is frequently done in times of natural disasters and is reported to be a simple procedure.

- Some hospitals have surgical vehicles that could be utilized.

- With further communication with the organ transplant community it may be possible to keep the inmate ventilated after a pronouncement of brain death so as to be able to transport him to a local transplant hospital.

- The issue is not insurmountable with open communication with experts in the field

Transplant Hospital Apprehensions

- The media involvement will likely sculpt the decision of local transplant hospitals as to whether they will accept condemned donations.

- There are a number of experts willing to consult with the hospitals now to come to an amiable decision concerning such donations.

SUMMARY OF CONFLICTS

Organ Donations From Willing Inmates

<u>Why living organ donation from willing prisoners is not occurring now:</u>

- Medical industry guidelines from decades past discourage the use of inmates for organ donations due to:

- Prisoners are at high risk for infectious diseases such as HIV and Hepatitis

- Testing for diseases is not 100% accurate.

- Some believe the prisoners cannot give appropriate consent to donation.

- There is racial and socio-economic inequality within prisons that will raise concerns

- Donation from prisoners may cause a stigma on organ donation in general

- Prison authorities are reluctant to allow it due to:

- Prison safety and security issues

- Logistics

- Transplant community dissuasion

Prisoners are at High Risk for Infectious Diseases

(See 'Chapter 3: Prisoners Are Disgusting)

<u>There is a high rate of prevalence for HIV and Hepatitis in prisons that increases the risk of transmission from potential donor to recipient</u>

- Prisoners are 2 ½ times more likely to be infected with HIV/AIDS[139] and other infectious diseases.

- However, other populations around the U.S. have much higher prevalence rates, such as major cites like NYC, Miami, & DC[140]

- The African American community is 1 ½ times more likely to be infected than prisoners.

- Yet the transplant community seeks to increase donation rates in these populations.

Testing for Infection is Not 100% Accurate

(See 'Chapter 4: Testing Prisoners for Infectious Disease')

<u>Without 100% assurance that an inmate is not infectious, the transplant community does not want to consider such donations.</u>

- Most concern relates to a "window period" between infection and detection where there may be a false negative.

- Previous testing only detected the antibody to the virus, which could take up to several months to detect after infection.

- Modern testing capabilities can detect the actual virus within 5 days of infection.

- As one Department of Corrections HIV/HEP Prevention Coordinator acknowledged: "If a person has had both antibody and viral RNA testing and both are negative, there is no reason to believe that such person's organs, tissue, or blood products are infected with any communicable disease of interest." [141]

Can Inmates Give Appropriate Consent?

(See 'Chapter 5: Can Prisoners Even Consent to Organ Donation?')

<u>Due to prior coercions related to experimentations on prisoners, and the nature of prison, some believe that prisoners cannot give true voluntary consent to donate organs.</u>

- In the 50's-70's prisoners "consented" to be used for medical experimentation such as the effects of radiation on testicular function. [142]

- However, such "consent" was coerced through paid inducements to participate and was therefore exploited.

- Prisoners are a vulnerable class of people, but courts have ruled that they can give appropriate consent, even to a point of refusing Life-sustaining treatments [143]

- If an inmate has chosen to donate an organ, has been given the same info and counseling as all other potential organ donors and is not receiving any inducements to participate, appropriate consent can be obtained.

Prisoner Donations May Stigmatize other Donations

Due to prior abuses by prison officials, some believe that the use of prisoners as donors may dissuade other donations, thus having the effect of wiping out altruistic donations.

- This is strictly a voluntary process that would be governed by the application of true consent without incentives.

- The inmate must broach the subject himself and prove that he is altruistically making the choice to donate his organs.

- Prior negative publicity (in the 80's) had an entirely different landscape of donor difficulties.(Less than 30k on waiting lists)

- Proposal already has wide public support.(65.4% locally)

- Other inmate–assisted programs (i.e. forest fire fighting, natural disaster support) do not deter public participation.

- The fact is that nobody knows what sort of impact such a policy may have on existing organ donation efforts.

- Any proposals for change usually engender opposition where every effort is made to decipher reasons something will not work.

- It's possible that the fresh light placed on organ donations upon the allowance of prisoners to donate may serve to raise awareness for the issue, prompting non–prisoners to learn of the dire necessity of such donations in the U.S.

Prison Safety Issues

Because organ donations would necessarily take place outside of prison grounds, there is some concern that inmates may use

<u>donations as an elaborate means of escape or that the public may in some other way be in danger.</u>

- Prisoners leave the prison grounds daily for authorized medical treatments. Prison security officials have specific protocols that ensure the publics safety during these events.

- Prisons know the behaviors of inmates under its watch and would likely have a feel for any inmate that should not be granted the ability to donate due to specific concerns.

- If necessary, prisons can simply allow donations to be made only by those who meet a certain security classification.

- In the case of death row inmates, arrangements are made to procure organs on the prison grounds or transferring the executed inmate once he has been pronounced dead.

LETTER TO STATE LEGISLATORS

To: The Honorable

Re: Prisoner Organ & Tissue Donation Bill Sponsorship

Dear

I am one of a large number of your constituents who believes strongly in the need to **allow healthy and willing prisoners the right to be registered as potential organ and bone marrow donors** in this state. As many of your constituents are dying for lack of a matching healthy donor, the inability of willing inmates to register is needlessly costing the lives of many of your voters.

Recently, other states have begun looking into their laws governing organ donation with respects to prisoners. Utah, after a **unanimous** passing in both House and Senate, has just passed the first legislation giving inmates the right to sign up to donate organs and tissue after death. This new law clarified a previous ambiguity in the Uniform Anatomical Gift Act that created uncertainty about allowing prisoners to donate – one that likewise exists in your state's Act. By adding this law, countless lives will be saved that would have been lost otherwise.

The concerns that have prevented over 2 million inmates from being able to donate are now woefully outdated. The transplant community discouraged prisoner donations in the early 1990's due to concerns over infectious diseases and inadequate testing at the time, as well as concerns over coercion of vulnerable prisoners. They continue to deny this opportunity for those same reasons today, even though these concerns have been abated.

The following is a brief outline of the transplant community concerns and how these have been addressed:

"There is an increased risk of infectious disease in the prison setting."

- True, but misleading. Many major U.S. cities have much higher rates of infection than prisons. For example, Washington D.C. has an infection rate for HIV and AIDS that is six times greater then the prison system. The African American population of prison-aged men has almost twice as many HIV/AIDS infected than do prisons. Prisoners are a high-risk group, but they are not even close to being the greatest risk.

- To follow the same reasoning that the transplant community expresses to reject organ donation from prisoners, the transplant community would likewise disallow organ donations from the entire populations of many U.S. cities, and especially from all African Americans. On the contrary, many of these populations are actually regions of focus for the transplant community to increase organ donations within these areas.

"Testing for infectious disease is not 100% accurate and therefore prisoners should be excluded."

Problem:

In the early 90's, when the transplant community first made this determination, testing was in its relative infancy. There was no way to test for the virus itself, so they had to test for antibodies to the virus, which oftentimes didn't show up in sufficient quantities to detect until months after the infection. The results were many false negatives and the spread of disease.

Solved:

A decade ago testing improved to be able to detect the virus itself, bringing the window period between infection and detection from months to days. This has continued to improve from there, to the point that one prison HIV/AIDS specialist has stated, "If both ...

"Prisoners are a vulnerable class of people who should be protected from making such a drastic decision as donating an organ. Prisoners cannot truly consent to donation."

Problem:

Prior to 1977, prisoners were used for all manner of medical research. By 1972, the pharmaceutical industry was doing more than 90 percent of their experimental testing on prisoners. Prisoners were actually lining up to volunteer for these experiments because they were given inducements to participate that were oftentimes so great, relatively speaking, that their participation in the programs was virtually coerced. This led the government to intercede to guarantee that prisoners were protected from such potentially harmful abuses, and led others to believe that prisoners could not truly give consent.

Solved:

With organ donation, no incentives to participate are offered. While it is rare that an inmate will choose to undergo invasive procedures without some sort of financial inducements, there are many who are willing to give up an organ to save a life. They do so for reasons separate from prison life.

Prisoners can consent to other medical treatments, including life-ending choices. There are guidelines designed to obtain this consent appropriately. If an inmate has chosen to donate an organ, has been given the same info and counseling as all other potential organ donors and is not receiving any inducements to participate, appropriate consent can be obtained.

There is an immense inmate population in the U.S. who would like nothing better that to atone for some bad choices in life by saving a human life. The only thing preventing this from happening is the outdated concerns of a slow to evolve transplant community and little legal clarity.

Organ donation creates an opportunity for prisoners to give back to the community whose social norms have been violated and it provides an opportunity to help a fellow citizen who desperately needs help. Cultivating such a generosity of spirit can do much to rehabilitate criminals conditioned by a life of hardship who think only of themselves. The more that is being done to prepare an inmate for a positive reentry into the community benefits all involved.

Would you be willing to sponsor enabling legislation that would allow willing disease-free inmates to be registered as organ and bone marrow donors in your state, as Utah has just successfully done? Such legislation will result in actual saved lives of your constituents as well as potentially setting a pattern for other states to follow that will have a ripple effect of lives saved nationwide. There can be no higher legislation than that.

Thank you for your time and consideration of this issue, and for the fine work you do for the citizens of this state.

Sincerely,

Go to www.gavelife.org for more info.

INFO FOR STATE LEGISLATORS

Sample bill, as introduced and passed unanimously by the 2013 Utah state legislature.

**Suggested additions are underlined and italicized **

HB26

Inmate Organ Donation Act
2013 General Session
State of Utah

This bill provides for inmates to voluntarily donate their organs _while living or_ posthumously.

Highlighted Provisions:

This bill:

Requires the Utah Department of Corrections to provide a document of gift form at an inmate's request, indicating desire to make an anatomical gift _while living or_ if the inmate dies while in the custody of the department;

Requires the department to maintain a record of an inmate's anatomical gift determination;

Provides that the department may release to an organ procurement organization the names of all inmates who indicate they intend to make an anatomical gift.

Be it enacted by the legislature of the state of Utah:

Section 1. Section 64–13–44 is enacted to read:

63-13-44. *Living or* Posthumous Organ Donations by Inmates.

1) As used in this section:
   a) "Document of gift" has the same meaning as in Section 26-28-102.
   b) "Sign" has the same meaning as in Section 26-28-102.

2) Rule
   a) The Utah Department of Corrections shall make available to each inmate a document of gift form that allows an inmate to indicate the inmate's desire to make an anatomical gift *while living or* if the inmate dies in the custody of the department.
   b) If the inmate chooses to make an anatomical gift *while living or* after death, the inmate shall complete a document of gift in accordance with the requirements of Title 26, Chapter 28, Revised Uniform Anatomical Gift Act.
   c) The department shall maintain a record of the document of gift that an inmate provides to the department.

3) Notwithstanding Title 63G, Chapter 2, Government Records Access and Management Act, the department may, upon request, release to an organ procurement organization, as defined in Section 26-28-102, the names and addresses of all inmates who complete and sign the document of gift form indicating they intend to make an anatomical gift.

Contact Info for Successful Bill Sponsors

Chief Sponsor:
Steven Eliason
seliason@le.utah.gov

801-673-4748
815 Grambling Way
Sandy, Utah 89094

Senate Sponsor:
Margaret Dayton
mdayton@le.utah.gov
801-221-0623
97 N. Westview Drive
Orem, Utah 84058

PROPOSED PRISON POLICY CHANGE

TO INCLUDE PRISONER ORGAN AND TISSUE DONATION

AS ADOPTED BY THE TEXAS DEPARTMENT OF CRIMINAL JUSTICE
POLICY E-31.2

(**Suggested additions are <u>underlined</u> and italicized**)

ORGAN OR TISSUE DONATION

Purpose:

To ensure uniformity of eligibility of offenders for voluntary access to organ or tissue donation.

Policy:

I. The Texas Department of Criminal Justice (TDCJ) will make voluntary *living or posthumous* organ or tissue donations available to offenders at the TDCJ Hospital at Galveston. The consent for organ or tissue donation, as well as charges incurred in the preliminary testing and the actual donation process, are the sole responsibility of the donor, donor recipient, and organization financially responsible for the donation (including lab work, shipping and all hospital charges.)

II. During the intake process, each offender will be offered an opportunity to sign a "Gift of Life" Tissue and Organ Donor Form (Attachment A). This will allow tissue and organ donation for transplantation purposes only, *if the inmate chooses to make a living donation or* in the event of the death while in custody. Offenders who do not wish to make a decision at the time of intake may do so later through a request to Medical Records. If the offender wishes to rescind the gift, he/she will write "revoked" on the form, sign with a date/time and the signature witnessed.

III. All requests for offender participation in organ and tissue donation must be originated from the physician managing the organ recipient transplant team. Access to the offender housing assignment and facility personnel will occur through the TDCJ Division Director for Health Services or designee.

IV. The transplantation team will be responsible for informed consent in writing. All donations a free and voluntary. The offender will receive no award or compensation in any kind for his donation, including but not limited to preferred treatment by the TDCJ or improved opportunity for parole. An offender may refuse a donation at any time or consent to a donation as long as he/she is mentally competent, and this refusal or consent will not affect reward or penalty for having done so. All consents must include the potential organ of donation and whether the donation is to occur while the offender is alive or at death.

V. The transplant team coordinator may not initially communicate directly with the offender. The transplant team coordinator must contact the TDCJ Division Director for Health Services or designee to obtain permission and clearance to communicate with the offender. The Division Director for Health Services or designee will, in turn, communicate and coordinate the request with the UTMB or Texas Tech medical director as warranted.

VI. All organ or tissue harvesting will occur at the TCDJ Hospital at Galveston. If the organ or tissue harvesting technology is not available at that hospital, the Division Director for Health Services may authorize the organ or tissue harvesting to be done at a Texas facility other than the TDCJ Hospital at Galveston, on a case-by-case basis.

VII. TDCJ will absorb the transportation costs of the donor between the assigned facility and the TDCJ Hospital at Galveston as well as normal cost of operation security at the hospital. If the tissue or organ harvesting is authorized at another facility, then the donor recipient or organization responsible for payment must bear the transportation and security costs. The TDCJ will provide an estimate for these anticipated costs and payment must be received prior to the movement of the donor from his/her assigned facility.

G.A.V.E. MISSION STATEMENT:

G.A.V.E. is a non-profit organization dedicated to groups who have been needlessly prohibited from donating healthy organs and tissue to those who need them to survive. It is our endeavor to research this ban and to educate the transplant community and the general public of the modern realities and benefits of organ donations from all needlessly banned but healthy individuals. We are committed to organizing and empowering all who are healthy and wish to become organ or tissue donors with the ability to donate and to provide others an increased chance at survival

References

References

1: The History of Organ Transplantation & the Donor Shortage

1 Organizacion Nacional de Taplantes, http://www.ont.es/newsletter/newsletter2008.pdf

2 http://www.huffingtonpost.com/2010/04/27/new-york-to-be-first-orga_n_554234.html

3 MEPSBack Europe Organ Donor Card, BBC News, April 22, 2008, http://news.bbc.co.uk/2/hi/health/7358789.stm

4 Brain Death and Transplantation: The Japanese, Medscape, April 25, 2000, http://www.medscape.com/viewarticle/408769

5 http://www.ramadanfoundation.com/organ.htm

6 http://www.uktransplant.org.uk/ukt/how_to_become_a_donor/religious_perspectives/leaflets/islam_and_organ_donation.jsp

7 Frequently Asked Questions About the Halachic Organ Donor (HOD) Society, http://www.hods.org/English/about/faqhods.asp

8 Health System Reform in China, The Lancet, October 20, 3008, http://www.thelancetglobalhealthnetwork.com/wp-content/uploads/Health-System-reform-in-China-CMT-11.pdf

9 "Article by Dr. Tom Treasure in the Journal of the Royal Society of Medicine", http://www.dafoh.org/Article_by_Dr.php

10 China fury at Organ Snatching 'Lies', BBC News, June 28, 2001, http://news.bbc.co.uk/1/hi/world/Americas/1411389.stm

11 Illegal Human Organ Trade from Executed Prisoners in China, http://www1.american,edu/ted/prisonorgans.htm

12 Cash for Kidneys, Gary S. Becker and Julio Elias. Wall Strret Journal, C1 (Jan. 18, 2014). See also: WSJ Letters to the Editor in response to id. – (Jan. 22, 2014, A17).

13 The Red Market: On the Trail of the Worlds Organ Brokers, Bone Thieves, Blood Farmers, and Child Traffickers, Scott Carney

14 http://organharvestinvestigation.net/report20070131.htm#_Toc160145122

References

15 China's New Rules on Organs, BBC, April 7, 2007, http://news.bbc.co.uk/2/hi/asia-pacific/6534363.stm

2: Organ Donation and Prisoners

16 United Network for Organ Sharing (UNOS), http://www.unos.org

17 California Transplant Donor Network - Resources, http://www.ctdn.org/resources_public.php#Statistics

18 Johns Hopkins Leads First 12-Patient, Multi-Center "Domino Donor" Kidney Transplant, Feb. 16, 2009 http://www.hopkinsmedicine.org/Press_Releases/2009/02_16_09.html

19 Kidney Donations Connect Strangers in Chain of Life Forged by Transplants, The Star Ledger, June 5, 2009 http://www.nj.com/news/index.ssf/2009/06/kidney_donations_connect_stran.html

20 Massive Transplant Effort Pairs 13 Kidneys to 13 Patients, Cnn.com, 2009 http://www.cnn.com/2009/HEALTH/12/14/kidney.transplant/index.html

21 First 16-Patient, Multicenter 'Domino Donor' Kidney Transplant, Science Daily, July 11, 2009 http://www.sciencedaily.com/releases/2009/07/090707183138.htm

22 See John Hopkins University Study (2010), Reviewed 80,347 living kidney donations between 1994 - 2009.

23 Encouraging Bone Marrow Transplants for Unrelated Donors, Mark F. Anderson, 54 U. Pitt L. Rev. 477, 482 (1993)

24 See WHO Guiding Principles on human cell, tissue, and organ transplantation, Annexed to World Health Organization, 2008. http://apps.who.int/gb/ebwha/pdf_files/A62/A62_15-en.pdf

25 They administer The Organ Procurement and Transplantation Network (OPTN) under contract with HRSA of the U.S. Department of Health and Human Services.

26 The Neuroscience of Fair Play: Why We (Usually) Follow the Golden Rule, Donald W. Pfaff

References

3: Prisoners Are Disgusting

27 AIDS in Prison: Judicial Indifference to the AIDS Epidemic in Correctional Institutions Threatens the Constitutionality of Incarceration, D. Stuart Sowder, 37 N.Y.L. Sch. L. Rev. 663, 666 (1992)

28 Id. At 668

29 Guidelines for Preventing Transmission of Human Immunodeficiency Virus through Transplantation of Human Tissue and Organs, MMWR 43 (RR-8); 1-17, May 20, 1994 – (Excluding 'Inmates of Correctional Systems' as organ donors: "This exclusion is to address issues such as difficulties with informed consent and increased prevalence of HIV in this population.")

30 Recommendations for the Deferral of Current and Recent Inmates of Correctional Institutions as Donors of Whole Blood, Blood Components, Source Leukocytes, and Source Plasma, Kathryn C. Zoon, PhD, Director, Center for Biologics Evaluation and Research (June 8, 1995)

31 Bureau of Justice Statistics Bulletin, HIV in Prisons, 2001-08 – See Methodology, AIDS in the U.S. resident population.

32 See http://www.organdonor.gov, click on "Grant Activities" under Research, Best Practices & Legislation.

33 Biovigilence in the United States, Public Health Service, 60 (2009)

34 Kidneys Transplanted Between HIV Patients, Mike Stobbe, Associated Press

35 Organ Donors with AIDS Accepted, Oregonian A2 (4/12/11)

4: Testing for Infectious Disease

36 Hepatitis & Liver Disease, Dr. Melissa Palmer (2004), P. 110

37 AIDS in Prison: Judicial Indifference to the AIDS epidemic in Correctional Institutions Threatens the Constitutionality of Incarceration, D. Stuart Sowder, 37 N.Y.L. Sch. L. Rev. 663, 666 (1992)

38 Id. At 668

39 http://www.cdc.gov, 'Fast Facts'

References

40 Guidelines for Preventing HIV through Transplantation of Human Tissue and Organs, CDC Recommendations and Reports, May 20, 1994 /43(RR-8); 1-17

41 Donor-Derived Disease Transmission Events in the United States: Data Reviewed by OPTN/UNOS Disease Transmission Advisory Committee, M.G. Ison, et al. American Journal of Transplantation 2009; 9: 1929-1935

42 CDC Urges New HIV Testing for Donors, Laura Landry, Wall Street Journal, 6/19/13

5: Can Prisoners Even Consent to Organ Donation?

43 States in which some medical research was conducted on prisoner volunteers during at least some period of time after 1970 include Michigan, Montana, California, Texas, Indiana, Connecticut, Missouri, Oklahoma, Illinois, Florida, Georgia, Massachusetts, New Jersey, Ohio, Rhode Island, Nebraska, and Kentucky. Non-therapeutic biomedical research was conducted in state prisons in the following states in 1975: California, Indiana, Maryland, Michigan, Montana, Texas, Virginia, Connecticut, and Massachusetts.

44 Bibeau v Pacific Northwest Research Foundation, 980 F. Supp 349 (1997), U.S. Dist. Court Ninth District

45 Abbdulaziz v City of Philadelphia, 2001 U.S. Dist. Lexis 16972, U.S. Dist. Court Eastern Dist of PA

46 Past Medical Testing on Humans Revealed, Mike Stobbe, AP medical writer, February 27, 2011

47 The Prison As Laboratory: Experimental Medical Research on Inmates Is On the Rise, Talvi, S. J.

References

48 The National Research Act, approved July 12, 1974, established a program partly for behavioral research and a mechanism for the development of standards and procedures for protection of human subjects involved in biomedical and behavioral research. Title II of the Act provides in Part A for the establishment of a National Commission for the Protection of Human Subjects of Biomedical and Behavioral Research. This was followed by subpart C on November 16, 1978, "Additional Protections Pertaining to Biomedical & Behavioral Research Involving Prisoners as Subjects", restricting research on prisoners (45 C.F.R. 46.301 – 46.306).

49 Professor Patricia King, a strong opponent of research on prisoners.

50 See 45 C.F.R. §§ 46.301–306 (1985)(HHS) "Additional protections pertaining to biomedical and behavior research involving prisoners as subjects."

51 28 C.F.R. §§ 512.10–22 (1985)(BOP)

52 Consent to Treatment, A Practical Guide, Fay A. Rozofsky (2d Edition 1990), 216–219

53 OAR 291-124-0080 Patient Rights (Inmate Health), Sec. 2: Informed Consent

54 Thor v. Superior Court, 855 P.2d 375, 5 Cal. 4th 725 (1993)

55 ORS 127.850 § 3.08 "No less than fifteen (15) days shall elapse between the patients' initial oral request and the writing of a prescription…"

6: China's Bad Example

56 In response to New York Times editorial, "Giving Life After Death Row" by Christian Longo. (Op-ed, March 6, 2011)

57 Whitney Hinkle, Giving Until it Hurts, Prisoners are Not the Answer to the National Organ Shortage – 35 Ind L. Rev. 593, 598 (2002)

58 Health System Reform in China, The Lancet, October 20, 3008, http://www.thelancetglobalhealthnetwork.com/wp-content/uploads/Health-System-reform-in-China-CMT-11.pdf

59 "Article by Dr. Tom Treasure in the Journal of the Royal Society of Medicine", http://www.dafoh.org/Article_by_Dr.php

References

60 Prospect of Discussions on Prisoners' Organs for Sale in China, Cesar Chelala – 350 Lancet 1307, 1307 (1997)

61 Testimony Before the Senate Foreign Relations Committee, China: Transplantation of Executed Prisoners' Organs, May 4, 1995 – Mike Jendrzejczyk, Director, Human Rights Watch/Asia

62 FBI Hears Report that China Executes Prisoners to Sell Organs, Les Blumenthal – Fresno Bee, October 23, 1997, at A8

63 Primetime: Blood Money: Black Market for Kidneys from Chinese Prisoners – (ABC News television broadcast October 15, 1997)

64 Organs for Sale: China's Growing Trade and Ultimate Violation of Human Rights – Hearing before Senate Subcommittee on International Operations and Human Rights, Committee on International Relations, 107th Cong. 24 (2001)

65 Doctor Says He Took Transplant Organs from Executed Chinese Prisoners, Craig G. Smith – New York Times, June 29, 2001, at A10. – See also US v Wang and YU, 1999 U.S. Dist. LEXIS 2913 (US Dist. Court– S. Dist. Of NY)

66 Panel Told of Organ Harvests on Executed Chinese Inmates, Bill Nichols – USA Today, June 28, 2001, at A12

67 See supra note 8.

68 Outraged at China's Sale of Organs, Dan Burton – Indianapolis Star, June 29, 1998, at A5

69 Death Row Inmates as Organ Donors: China's Source of Body Organs for Transplantation, Allison K. Owen – 5 Ind. Int'l & Comp. Law Review 495, 499–502 (1995)

70 Death Row is Organ Source, China Admits, Mark Magnier and Alan Zarembo – L.A. Times, November 18, 2006, at A1

71 China Say's to Ban Sale of Human Organs, Lindsay Beck – Reuters, March 28, 2006

72 Rethinking the Prohibition of Death Row Prisoners as Organ Donors, Donny J. Perales – 34 St. Mary's L. J. 687, 701 (2003)

References

73 China to Stop Taking Inmates' Organs, Laurie Burkitt, Wall Street Journal, April, 2012

See Also: China Bans Sale of Human Transplant Organs, Associated Press, March 28, 2006; See also Chinese Ministry of Health Homepage, http://www.moh.gov.cn/

74 Amnesty International USA, People's Republic of China: Executed "According to Law"? The Death Penalty in China http://www.amnestyusa.org/abaolish/document.do.?id=806E474afd57dc5980256e5c00688e40

75 See id. See also Formula to Stop Illegal Organ Trade: Presumed Consent Laws and Mandatory Reporting Requirements for Doctors, Sheri R. Glaser – 12 Hum Rts. Brief 20 (2005)

76 Cadaveric Organ Donation and Consent: A Comparative Analysis of the U.S., Japan, Singapore and China, Sean R. Fitzgibbons – 6 ILSA J. Int'l & Comp L. 73, 101 (1999)

77 Quandary in U.S. Over Use of Organs of Chinese Inmates, Craig S. Smith – New York Times, November 11, 2001

78 See supra note 2

79 The Bottom Line of Organ Donating, Ellen Goodman – Abilene Reporter-News, March 10, 1998

80 China's Execution, Inc., Erik Baard & Rebecca Cooney – Village Voice, May 8, 2001

81 See supra note 1; See also supra note 9

82 See supra note 7

83 U.S. Department of Health and Human Services (DHHS) oversees the Organ Procurement and Transplantation Network (OPTN), which has contracted the United Network of Organ Sharing (UNOS) to organize and maintain organ transplant guidelines.

84 42 U.S.C. § 274 (a) (2000)

85 JoNell Alleccia, MSNBC.com, April 21, 2011 (Citing a UNOS representative's opinion.)

References

7: Doesn't Lethal Injection Kill the Organs?

86 Todlicke Injektion, (http://www.todesstrafe.de/thema/geschichte/geschichte/toedliche_injektion.php)

87 Capital Punishment U.K.: Lethal Injection (http://www.richard.clark32.btinternet.co.uk/injection.html)

88 Baze v. Rees, 128 S. Ct. 1520 (2008)

89 The surgical removal of the organs occurs while the patient has an intact circulation and is mechanically ventilated. Once the organs are removed, the ventilator and cardiac monitor are removed.

90 See: American Medical Association Opinion 2.06 – Capital Punishment. Re: Physician Participation. See also:
- Physicians' Willingness to Participate in the Process of Lethal Injection for Capital Punishment, Neil J. Farber et al., 135 Annals Internal Medicine 884, 886 (2001)
- Physicians' Attitudes about involvement in Lethal Injection for Capital Punishment, Neil J. Farber et al., 160 Archives of Internal Med. 2912, 2912 (noting that in a recent survey of physicians, more than half approved of the AMA's disallowed medical actions involving capital punishment.)
- Physician Participation in Capital Punishment, Dr. David Waisel, Mayo Clinic Proceedings, September 2007;82(9): 1073–1080

91 See Affidavit of Terry Collins, ODRC Director under U.S. District Court for the Southern District of Ohio, Case No. 2:04-cv-1156, specifying the changes to Ohio's lethal injection protocols. (One single drug: 5 grams of thiopental sodium.)

92 See "Declaration of Stephen Sinclair", Superintendent– 3/1/10. Washington State Penitentiary. See also Wash DOC Policy 490.200, Capital Punishment, revised 3/8/10.

8: Will Physicians Participate?

93 Hippocrates, Columbia Encyclopedia, 6th Edition

94 The Hippocratic Oath 10, L. Edelstein (1943)

References

95 See full American Medical Association Code of Ethics; Opinion E-2.06 @ http://www.ama.com

96 Id. – Physicians are also allowed by the AMA to help the condemned to relieve anxiety and suffering in anticipation of their execution.

97 Id.

98 Compassion in Dying v. Washington, 79 F3d 790 (1994)(9th Circuit US Court of Appeals)

99 Physician-Assisted Suicide and the Right to Die with Assistance, 105 Harv. L.Rev. 2021, 2021 n. 7 (1992) According to the same survey, one doctor in four said he had been asked by a patient for assistance in ending his life.

100 ORS 137.476, (paraphrased) Any assistance rendered in an execution carried out by a licensed health care professional or a nonlicensed medically trained person is not cause for disciplinary measures or regulatory oversight by any board, commission or agency created by this state or governed by state law that oversees or regulates the practice of health care professionals...

101 58 Fed. Reg. 4898 (1993)

102 28 CFR Part 26

103 Physicians' Willingness to Participate in the Process of Lethal Injection for Capital Punishment, Neil J. Farber et al., 135 Annals Internal Medicine 884, 886 (2001)

104 Physicians' Attitudes about involvement in Lethal Injection for Capital Punishment, Neil J. Farber et al., 160 Archives of Internal Med. 2912, 2912 (noting that in a recent survey of physicians, more than half approved of the AMA's disallowed medical actions involving capital punishment.)

105 Dr. David Waisel, Physician Participation in Capital Punishment, Mayo Clinic Proceedings, September 2007;82(9): 1073-1080

9: Is Prisoner Organ Donation Ethical?

106 History of Ethics, Vernon J. Bourke, 8 (1962)

107 Nicomachean Ethics, 1105b20 – 1106a11, Aristotle

References

108 Online article on Longo and Phillips efforts to donate from death row, JoNel Allecia – Poll Taken 4/21/11 –

109 Salem, Oregon newspaper poll in response to article of Longo's organ donation efforts

Poll taken 12/16/09

110 Portland, Oregon ABC affiliate poll in response to Longo news coverage – Poll taken between 3/11/11 – 3/20/11 – Additional polls have asked the question: "Should prisoners be allowed to make living donations?" (See MSNBC, KATU2, KOIN6, KPTV12 polls, and various online forums and blogs)

111 Prisoner Should be able to Donate, Courtney Graham – McGill Daily, March 28, 2011

112 Ethical Issues in the Practice of Psychiatry, Edward M. Hundert – The Harvard Guide of Psychiatry, p. 750

113 Dying vs. Washington, 850 Fsupp 1454 @ 1464 (1994)

114 My Fight for Birth Control, Sanger, M, 1931

115 Terminating Life, Mccuen, G.E., and Boucher, T., p.60 (1985).

116 Id @ 76

117 Oregon Administrative Rules, (OAR) 291-078-0005 (3)(d), Community Services

118 Code of Medical Ethics, AMA, 1996, Section 7

119 Reconstruction in Philosophy, 132–133, Dewey (New York: Mentor 1953)

11: Can Prisoners' Traits 'Live On' in Donated Organs?

120 Organ Transplants and Cellular Memories, by Gary E. Schwartz, PhD, Paul Pearsall, PhD and Linda G. Russek, PhD, Nexus Magazine, Volume 12, Number 3 (April – May 2005).

121 Name has been changed to respect the anonymity of the recipient.

122 The building blocks of proteins, including antibodies, are amino acids. There are 20 commonly found amino acids. An amino acid is linked together by peptide bonds, which create a "peptide".

References

12: Recent Developments in Prisoner Organ Donation

123 House Panel Nixes Plan for Inmate Organ Transplants, Strait, J, St Louis Post-Dispatch, April 10, 1998, at C3.

124 Operation Blue, Ultra: Dion – The Donation Inmate Organ Network, Bartz, CE, Kennedy Institute of Ethics Journal. 13(1):37–43

125 "Giving Life After Death Row", New York Times Op-Ed Article by Christian M. Longo– March 6, 2011

Conclusion

126 http://www.MSNBC.com, Killers Quest, Allow Organ Donation After Execution. – JoNel Allecia, 4/21/11

127 Her name and circumstances have been changed to ensure anonymity.

Summary of Conflicts: Organ Donations from the Condemned

128 The Hippocratic Oath 10, L. Edelstein (1943)

129 Physicians' Willingness to Participate in the Process of Lethal Injection for Capital Punishment, Neil J. Farber et al., 135 Annals Internal Medicine 884, 886 (2001)

130 Also known as Nucleic Acid Amplification Testing. (NAAT)

131 See various online polls and blogs. Google: "Giving life after death row" Polls or Blogs – (70–80% avg. approval)
"Should death row prisoners be allowed to donate organs?" National: MSNBC.com Poll taken 4/21/11 (Yes: 77%, No: 12% – 85,000 participants) (See JoNel Alleccia article) Local: KATU2 Portland, OR Poll taken 3/17/11 (Yes: 79%); Statesman Journal (Salem, OR newspaper) Poll taken 12/16/09. (Yes: 65.4%, No: 23.3%, Don't Know: 7%)

132 See 6/16/10 Oregonian article touting Anonymous Living Donor Program: 4 years of the program generated 7 kidneys.

133 Opinions on Capital Punishment, Executions, & Medical Science, Medicine and Law 4, (1985) 515–33, Jack Kevorkian

134 Baze v. Rees, 128 S. Ct. 1520 (2008)

References

135 See Oregonian 6/19/10, Utah's reasoning for discontinuing the use of the firing squad

136 2004 Amnesty International Report

137 See Uniform Anatomical Gift Act & United Network for Organ Sharing

138 ORS 137.473. "All executions shall take place within the enclosure of a Department of Corrections institution designated by the Director of the Department of Corrections"

Summary of Conflicts: Organ Donations from Willing Inmates

139 Bureau of Justice Statistics Bulletin, HIV in Prisons, 2001–08

140 CDC HIV Surveillance Report, 2008

141 Ann Shindo, PhD, Oregon Department of Corrections. Response to author regarding testing protocols of ODOC.

142 Bibeau v Pacific Northwest Research Foundation, 980 F. Supp 349 (1997), U.S. Dist. Court Ninth District

143 Thor v. Superior Court, 855 P.2d 375, 5 Cal. 4th 725 (1993)

www.ingramcontent.com/pod-product-compliance
Lightning Source LLC
Chambersburg PA
CBHW051343200326
41521CB00014B/2459